Open Management

Better work for a better world

The Teal Unicorn view of work
and management

Rob England and Dr. Cherry Vu

Teal Unicorn
The new way of working

Created by Two Hills Ltd (trading as Teal Unicorn™)
letterbox@twohills.co.nz
www.twohills.co.nz
PO Box 57-150, Mana
Porirua 5247
New Zealand

Two Hills
Sensible business practices

© Copyright Two Hills Ltd 2021

Foreword is Creative Commons Attribution-ShareAlike 3.0 Unported, attribution to Ed Morrison.
Published by Two Hills Ltd
First edition. (Version 1.5, December 2021)
First published 2021
Unless otherwise credited, all photos and diagrams are by the authors.
Jewellery images © Canstockphoto.com.
Cover image: pixabay
The moral rights of the authors are asserted.
All Rights Reserved. No part of this publication may be reproduced, stored in a retrieval system, or transmitted, in any form or by any means, electronic, mechanical, photocopying, recording or otherwise, without prior permission of the authors.
Although this book has been carefully prepared, neither the authors nor the publisher accepts any liability for damages caused by any error or omission of this book. We make no claim that the use of any aspect of this book will assure a successful outcome.
Use of any trademarks in this document is not intended in any way to infringe on the rights of the trademark holder.
The Two Hills logo, "Teal Unicorn", "Unicorn Management Model", and The Teal Unicorn logo are trademarks of Two Hills Ltd.
SAFe and Scaled Agile Framework are registered trademarks of Scaled Agile, Inc
ITIL and PRINCE2 are registered trademarks of Axelos Limited.

ISBN 9798778627758

Imprint: Independently published

Teal Unicorn™
Make work better
Better results, better lives, better society

In a hurry? Read **Part One**, 60 pages from **page 13**.

Contents

Foreword by Ed Morrison	1
About this book	8
Layout of the book	9
How to read this book	9
The agile Manager Community	10
Acknowledgements	12
Part One: EXPOSITION	13
Management practices	66
Part Two: EXPERIENCES	75
Narwhal Design, a tale of agility	79
Case studies	87
Vinh Duc: Self-organising	89
LOC: Reorganising	105
LINHPOHS: Precious time	119
ERICK: Real and effective	129
LamLuy: Working	135
Teal Unicorn in Vietnam	145
Part Three: ELABORATION	157
Open Work	159
Human Systems Adaptability	159
Humanity	160
Trust	161
Integrity	162
Values	162
Wholeness	164
Morality	164
Ethics	166
Authenticity	167
Vulnerable	167
Bullshit	168
Permissioning	169
Bad behaviour	170
Diversity	171
Inclusion	172
Psychological Safety	174

Human Resilience	175
Respect	176
Fun	176
Love	177
Systems thinking	179
Self-organising teams	180
Environment	180
Workplace	180
Healthy office	181
Remote work	182
Value network	183
Value stream	183
Planning	184
Bureaucracy	186
Adaptability	187
Fluidity	188
Failure	188
The J-curve	189
Imperfection	191
Work Safety	191
Resilience	192

Open Management   195

Middle managers	196
Managerial resistance	197
Scientific management	198
Measurement	199
Measuring people	201
Performance	203
Pressure	203
Punishment	204
Firing	205
Engagement	207
Patience	208
Humanistic management	209
Servant manager	210
Flip the hierarchy	211
Invitation	212
Authority	212
Transparency of management	213
Gemba	213
Decision making	215
Leadership	219
Organisation	219

Open Thinking	221
Agile	223
Navigational star	226
Vision	227
Social evolution	227
Laloux model	228
Teal	231
Reunification	231
Humanistics	233
The Lizard Brain	237
Environmental, Social, and Governance concerns	238
Stakeholder capitalism	239
Activist shareholders	240
Complexity	241
Complex adaptive systems	243
VUCA	245
Sense-making	246
Cynefin	246
Change is a permanent state	248
Learn more	251
The agile Manager (small "a")	255
Teal Unicorn	257
Make work better	258
Have fun	258

Testimonials

What people are saying about Teal Unicorn

[For] the first time in our company history, we have an improvement machine which helps to remove constraints and makes the workflow much faster. People start behaving differently, they work in a co-operative and supportive way toward a common goal.

– CEO, large manufacturer

I have changed my mind. I stop blaming people. I give my people a task with clear instructions. When something goes wrong, we all work together and find out the causes not pointing fingers at someone. That helps us to create a comfortable environment and positive thinking.

– Factory director

I see when my opinion and consciousness have changed, a lot of things changed. I can't describe it clearly, but after coming home from your training, I look at things clearer, more excited, more confident, and that inspires others. Then change happens every day. I go on making small changes and people continue to follow, I don't need to urge them.

- Company owner and CEO

What people said about the previous book, *The agile Manager (small a)*

Every organization needs to work out how to do whatever it does in a more agile way, but while many resources exist for implementing agile in technology organizations, less do so for traditional industries.

- Ben Kepes, professional board member, investor, commentator

When all the buzzwords become overwhelming, this is a book you can come to for a bit of clarity. Remember that dogma is the enemy of learning, and agile has a small "a"...

- Dawie Olivier, Chief Information Officer, Westpac NZ

I love what this book brought out in me professionally. The concepts and principles can be challenging yet I often re-visit and recommend this book.

- Lisa Andrews, Motivational Speaker

New ways of managing is no longer an option. Doing 'stuff' in a more agile manner is no longer an option. All you need to know to become a competent and capable agile manager is in this book.

- Karen Ferris, author of Game On! Change is Constant

It is hard to overstate how much fun I am having reading this book. I started a few weeks ago and have been reading a few pages each day, slowly realizing that this is a wonderful way to meditate on the decade that was and the decade that will be.

- Elijah Lovejoy, Co-Founder, Ondema

Foreword[1]

Over two decades ago, Canadian environmental scientist Thomas Homer-Dixon wrote an important book: *The Ingenuity Gap*. He pointed to the growing gap between the ingenuity we need and the ingenuity we produce. Solutions to the accelerating complexity of our world demands more ingenuity from us: we need to generate more ingenious solutions. Yet, our current approach to organizations, business, and economic policy stunts the supply.

Just one statistic underscores how we are stifling human ingenuity. In 2020, Gallup found that globally only 20% of workers feel engaged in their job. In what other system would we accept this level of performance? Imagine what would happen to Tesla, Toyota, or Ford if only one in five automobiles they produced actually worked as designed.

So, some early conclusions:

- We are wasting brainpower at an alarming level.

- We clearly have different standards operating for the stuff we produce, as opposed to the humans we manage.

- When it comes to Homer-Dixon's Ingenuity gap, we are moving too slowly. We are not adapting fast enough. It's a widespread cultural problem.

We can't say that we weren't warned.

---

[1] The Foreword is Creative Commons Attribution-ShareAlike 3.0 Unported License Ed Morrison 2021

Foreword

Thirty years before Homer-Dixon wrote his book -- over fifty years ago from today -- MIT scholar Donald Schön delivered the Reith lecture for the BBC[2]. Schön told us that we were moving from an era of relative calm to an era of turbulence. The industrial organizations and political institutions that had provided a sense of stability in the 1950s and 1960s were ill-suited for what was coming.

Schön set forth our challenge in clear terms. For us to adapt to constant change, we need to learn how both individuals and organizations learn. How do we design new learning systems so we can flourish in the "swampy lowlands" of complex problems? He dedicated the balance of his professional career to that question.

Schön asked us to think of businesses and government as learning systems. They each face learning challenges, but they are different. Businesses can be directed not just to produce things, but to address both functional needs (think of Christensen's "jobs to be done") and social challenges (producing clean energy, healthy food, affordable shelter, clean water, and, more recently, innovative mRNA vaccines). Because businesses are human systems, we can design them to generate and diffuse innovations more productively. We can do that, Schön advised, if we think about the structure of our networks. For government, among other innovations, he suggested that we need to design new types of learning systems that shift power from the center to the periphery.

Meeting both challenges requires a different type of learning. With his collaborator, Chris Argyris, Schön underscored the importance of "double loop learning", or what we can think of as adaptive learning. It's the type of learning that enables organizations to adapt and evolve. We can contrast adaptive learning to routine learning. An on-boarding process for new employees represents routine learning. A new employee learns how

---

[2] https://www.bbc.co.uk/programmes/p00h3xfh

to file expense reports, how to keep track of time, how to conform to brand guidelines, and so on: the routines of the business.

Adaptive learning is different. Here, we need a deeper, continuous inquiry. We need frequently to question the path we're on. Are our actions giving us the results we want? If not, we need to change course, change what we're doing. It's the essence of what has become "agile" thinking and doing.

If designing and implementing agile learning organizations were easy, we would have done it. Every organization could have adopted Senge's five disciplines by now, and we would be closing our Ingenuity Gap. Clearly, that is not happening. Embedding adaptive learning in an organization -- creating a "learning organization" -- is hard. The reason: we need to change the way people think, the way they behave, and the way they work together. We need to penetrate learning to the day-to-day experiences of individuals. We need specific skills people can learn, practice, and master. Translating a theory into skills and new "dynamic capabilities" is not easy. We don't learn to ride a bicycle by reading a book. We learn by doing.

Operating on a clean slate -- in a start-up mode -- the challenge is already tricky. What new routines are needed? What new heuristics? Inside an existing organization, the challenge is far more complex. As Argyris explained (in the 1980s), there are a wide range of defensive behaviors that slow the development of adaptive learning. Together, they can form a powerful immune response. This response, Argyris explained, shows up in the various forms of "politicking" within the organization. Participants quickly frame situations in win-lose terms. Competition overcomes collaboration. Mistrust displaces trust. Unquestioning obedience squeezes out informed dissent. Coalitions form to claim turf. The result: adaptive learning opportunities vanish.

Overcoming the resistance to adaptive learning is not easy. Because every organization is unique and operates in a different context, no standard model will work. We have to experiment and learn relentlessly. We need to think of both our systems and our next steps: zooming out and zooming in, as John Hagel suggests. And we must be humble. We are dealing with invisible knowledge flows moving through invisible networks. It's not rocket science. It's far harder. It's more like molecular biology.

The challenge of embedding adaptive learning falls directly on the doorstep of business. Why is that? As Schumpeter explained, the market economy provides powerful incentives to innovate. Yet, when we reflect on Homer-Dixon's Ingenuity Gap, we can see that business has been focused on the wrong measures: narrow financial metrics like hurdle rates, shareholder value, and quarterly earnings. The recent move to "stakeholder capitalism" may shift the dynamic, but it's not likely. A top-down declaration is not a movement. It fails to engage individuals in the organization. Changing the way people think, behave, and do work together involves designing powerful, customized learning experiences. That is missing from stakeholder capitalism so far.

As Mariana Massucatto has documented, business has been pointing their innovation capability at the wrong targets. We don't need more stuff; we need better (and likely less) stuff. We need dramatically more energy from renewable sources; packaging that doesn't destroy our oceans; products we can recycle in a circular economy; manufacturing that produces zero waste; education systems that are more flexible and customized. We need to operate within our planetary boundaries.

In other words, we need a vibrant Civic Economy to guide our Market Economy. The simplistic prescriptions of neoclassical economics have failed us. Unfettered markets create income inequalities that devour the democratic consensus that markets need to operate. This idea is not new. Before Adam Smith wrote *The Wealth of Nations*, he authored The

Theory of Moral Sentiments. We are social creatures, Smith explained, and empathy -- embedded in our morality -- is a natural part of our humanity. Our moral sentiments operate to guide markets to higher levels of shared prosperity.

If we have learned anything in the past thirty years it is this: markets, left alone and unregulated, can produce disastrous results. Greed has no stopping rules, unless through civic action we impose them. When we step back and allow greed to take over, both markets and nations fail. Robinson and Acemoglu in their marvelous book *Why Nations Fail* provide ample evidence.

Finding out how to design and guide the dynamic balance between the Market Economy and the Civic Economy will not be easy. This is the risk that Schön in 1970 pointed out. Neither government nor business is learning fast enough.

Now, 50 years later, the outlook is gradually changing. If the pandemic has any positive outcomes, they are likely embedded in the shifts taking place in how we work and organize ourselves. We are seeing the value of remote work and self-directed teams. Despite the pundits, no one has all the answers. In dynamic environments, there will never be best practices, only promising ones. Everyone is looking at the world through their own straw. Many experiments are underway to create more dynamic, agile organizations, and many different solutions are possible across this dancing landscape.

These solutions will likely share some common characteristics. They will be built on a culture of psychological safety, as Amy Edmondson has demonstrated. Ingenious solutions require complex, collective thinking. We cannot think together if we do not behave in ways that build trust and mutual respect. Trust powers the flow of knowledge through networks, and people cannot easily build trusting relationships in emotionally hostile environments. Fostering a psychologically safe workspace is common sense: the equivalent of putting the shower curtain on the inside of the bathtub.

Our solutions will also leverage the power of platforms, self-directed teams, networks, and ecosystems. Innovation is a process of recombining assets we already have in our networks. While we cannot manage this process too tightly, we can design and guide the platforms on which these interactions take place. We can embed protocols of adaptive learning on these platforms.

Our solutions will improve both the quantity and quality of the interactions we have among us: our conversations. Again, this insight is not new. Alan Webber, when he was an editor of the Harvard Business Review, wrote a prescient article in 1993[3]. He pointed to the power of our conversations as the way we generate and distribute our knowledge across our networks.

Understanding how this happens is not a trivial problem. I have spent over two decades identifying the simple rules that underlie complex collaborations. The good news is that we now know that complex collaborations emerge from conversations with a predictable structure. We can now teach the skills to design and guide these conversations. You can think of our work as an open-source operating system for collaborations. That step should help us narrow our Ingenuity Gap. If we can increase the volume and velocity of our collaborations, we will likely also increase the production of ingenious solutions.

A last word: in 1993, I set out to design a new approach to strategy, one designed for open, loosely connected networks. My journey has been

---

[3] https://store.hbr.org/product/what-s-so-new-about-the-new-economy/93109?sku=93109-PDF-ENG

difficult at times but enormously rewarding. I used Donald Schön and others as guides. As you set out to design what's next for yourself or your organization, here is what I can share. The road ahead is not well lit or paved. It's more a thin path or a poorly marked trail heading into the bush. To set out, as John Hagel has explained, you will need to overcome chronic fears and embrace the spirit of the explorer. You will need a core team of people to support your work. And you will need experienced guides to share their intuitions and insights. You hold in your hands a book from two of those guides. Before you set off on your own journey, read and reflect on what Rob and Cherry share with us.

    Ed Morrison
    Co-Author of *Strategic Doing*[4]

---

[4] https://strategicdoing.net

About this book

This book started life as an update of our book *The agile Manager (small a)*. We changed it so much that we changed the title and made it a new book. *The agile Manager* is a practical handbook that wants to be useful. This book, *Open Management* is a philosophical manifesto that wants to open minds and organisations. *The agile Manager* was the how, this is the why, and the who - who we need to be to make it possible.

The bad news is we now need to write both books, this one and an update to the other (next year), and you need to read both to share all we have learned. The good news is this book doesn't become massive or try to achieve two purposes. There is an overlap in ideas, but little duplication of content.

Parts of this book are going to seem bizarre to those of you new to those ideas. Stick with it. Even the most obvious ideas seem weird at first[5]. These aren't our original ideas. We - Teal Unicorn which is the brand of the authors Rob and Cherry - learned these "new[6] ways" from global communities of very clever people doing awesome things: Agile, Lean, Business Agility, Kaizen, Humanistics, Humanocracy, Sociocracy, Organisational Development, OpenSpace, Open Leadership, Transformational Leadership, Global Drucker Forum, Teal Network, Theory of Constraints, Kanban, DevOps, and more. The authors aren't expert in anything (except public policy, in which Cherry has a PhD). The ideas in this book are evident to us. We share them in the hope that they will become evident to you too. This is an opportunity for you and your organisation to make work better, more open.

---

[5] It is only kinky the first time. - Eddie Izzard.
[6] Many aren't new - what's new is they are now displacing conventional management

We proved them to ourselves with our clients[7]. We wrote a story about a hypothetical company called Narwhal Design, which you may find helpful to make it more concrete, and there are a number of client case studies with real proof points to reassure you.

Layout of the book

Foreword	1
About this book	8
Part One: EXPOSITION	13
Part Two: EXPERIENCES	75
Part Three: ELABORATION	157
Open Work	159
Open Management	195
Open Thinking	221
Learn more	251
Index	261

How to read this book

The main narrative of this book is found in "Part One". It is quite short, about 60 pages. We wrote it as a single exposition, a stream of consciousness, a single argument as to why we need to work differently. It is a bit different to most business books, but that fits the ethos of its message.

Everyone is in a hurry these days, so you may choose to read only Part One and get the message of the book. The rest is expanding on it. Part

---

[7] https://tealunicorn.com/clients/

Two tells the stories of our experiences with clients. Part Three is the endnotes referenced in Part One, which are more extensive than Part One! If you need elaboration, it is there. Even more elaboration and explanation of **how** to be open is in our other book *The agile Manager (small a)*.

Or maybe you are old school and will read all three parts of this book cover to cover. Expect only Part One to flow. Treat the rest as a collection of reflections and suggestions.

> Asides (additional commentary by the author) are indented and in a font like this. Those in a hurry can skip them.

A note on first-person pronouns: "I" refers to Teal Unicorn unless stated otherwise. Cherry and Rob are a tight team, happy to use a singular pronoun for the rest of this book to represent me (see what I did there). "We" means all of us including you, dear readers.

"Better ways" or "new ways"? "New ways of working" is a commonly used term. I used it in the previous book and up until now. I want to move to "better ways". "New" isn't always true, but "better" is (or else why do it?). My previous book and my website used "new". Bad decision. I went through this book and the website, and changed it.

The agile Manager Community

Thank-you for buying this book. You may like to be a part of the (small a) agile Manager community, which is open to those reading this book

Go to www.agilemanagers.club to find links to community pages and resources for this book, or Rob and Cherry can be found at www.tealunicorn.com.

You can find me on LinkedIn: "The agile Managers Club".

Rob is on Twitter @rob_england, and Cherry is @drcherryvu.

Drop in regularly: I will share fresh learning, and I will update parts of this book.

Join my mailing list: http://eepurl.com/gnW759.

About this book

Acknowledgements

A big thank-you to all those who improved the content, including Heidi Araya, Christophe de Boeck, Gill England, Ady Foot, James Gander, Stephen Hall, Wim Hoving, Jon Leighton, Guy Maslen, Gary Percival, Nick Pharo, Mark Smalley, Louis Stamford, Karen Thorpe, Aernout van den Burg, Dave van Herpen, Tim White.

A special thanks to Ed Morrison for writing the Foreword. Your beautifully crafted and learned prose doesn't show up my loose writing so much as enhance it.

It is hard to mention all the people who influenced this book. Thank-you to those past and present.

This book is dedicated to our tribes of supporters who energise and inspire us, in Vietnam, New Zealand, and around the world.

Cảm ơn tất cả các bạn rất nhiều!

Part One: EXPOSITION

The content of the book, presented with as much brevity as the Authors can muster, presenting the arguments for Open Management as a single narrative flow.

Building humanity at work, understanding systems, and adapting constantly to change are the strategies to make work better: better results, better lives at work, better society around us.

Conventional approaches to managing work are less effective now that the world is increasingly VUCA; and now that social beliefs about work are shifting. Both trends are accelerating.

The low-risk way forward is to advance in exploratory increments, experimenting at every step, embracing failure, learning always. In other words: adaptability, which is a combination of agility and resilience.

To achieve this, we make work *Open*: flexible, transparent, honest, inviting, inclusive, collaborative, liberated, connected, social, visionary, caring, embracing, safe, respectful, open-minded, expanding, free. And lighten up a bit, be friendly, have some fun.

To enable these different ways of working, we must change how we manage the work. Management must be equally open. If you don't change how you manage the work, people can't change how they work.

This isn't hypothetical. The body of anecdote and empirical evidence is growing. The authors' own experiences reinforce it. It works for us.

That's it, that's the book. If you get all that, we're done. Thanks for coming.

> The future is unpredictable and most people can be trusted. So obvious but yet so difficult.
>
> - Bjarte Bogsnes

Teal Unicorn's clients have tested those ideas and enjoyed great success with them, in a wide variety of contexts, from owner-manager to corporation, across logistics, banking, government, clothing, real estate, electronics, import, wholesale, retail, and service providers. Clients have tried tactics such as removing hierarchical management (moving to servant managers); allowing fluid team structures chosen by those doing the work; and changing reward systems to allow all to share in the success (creating more transparency and collaboration). Most of all they have tried being nice: treating people with respect, and setting them free from constraining systems.

The results have all been good: greater results, even during COVID, and - most of all - happier staff. I don't cherry-pick the stories we share and hide the bad outcomes: it always works, and quickly, for as long as it survives the politics (occasionally the organisation rejects the new ideas).

This book is for those who improve how we work, especially managers, coaches, and consultants. And all those working who want to take control of improvement, who want your own work to be better. Business, government, not-for-profit, around the world. If you are dissatisfied with how work works, and you are seeking better ways of working, this book will propose new directions for you to explore, and inspire you to go there to make work better.

"Horses", the established organisations with existing management structures, need this more than the seemingly-magical ones that already work in advanced ways, the "unicorns". If you can't fly or poo rainbows just yet, maybe you need to be a little different to be open to these ideas: a "zebra" - less conventional than a horse but nothing magical, just more open, more free.

You need this book because the world is changing too fast to continue to use conventional ways of working and managing, and thinking. What got you here won't get you there. Other books deal with better ways of working, but management is critical to unlock those better ways, to open work up. I operate in this space, and I want to share my ideas with you to help you.

> As Thomas Kuhn pointed out in his classic, *The Structure of Scientific Revolutions*, every model is flawed. Some can be useful for decades or even centuries, but eventually circumstances change and they become untenable. After a period of tumult, they collapse and a new paradigm emerges.
>
> - Greg Satell

There is a fresh enlightenment shaping societies that has been gaining pace since the 1960s. Within work, we see 20th Century scientific management is clinging on in the face of 21st Century humanistic management and business agility, or more broadly what I call Open Management and hence Open Work. I have deliberately named those management styles in terms of centuries, as this is one of those once-in-a-century step changes in thinking, just as scientific management was at the beginning of the 20th Century.

Making work better is an opening-up: it opens society to higher consciousness; it opens organisations to greater transparency and inclusion; it opens teams to collaboration; it opens us to self-examination, authenticity, and vulnerability, it opens us up to being human. I believe the transition is inevitable, but unfortunately, we all need to live through it. As the old curse says, "May you live in interesting times".

> An "open organization"—which I define as an organization that engages participative communities both inside and out—responds to opportunities more quickly, has access to resources and talent outside the organization, and inspires, motivates, and empowers people at all levels to act with accountability
>
> - Jim Whitehurst[8]

Imagine a workplace where you can bring your whole authentic self to work[p167]: where you don't have to hide your beliefs or your sexuality or your ethics[p166]. You can be open about yourself.

Imagine a workplace where the same standards of social interaction apply as anywhere else, where any behaviour that is unacceptable in any other social context is also unacceptable at work, such as shouting, bullying, patronizing, or prejudice.

Imagine a workplace where people care about each other as much as they do in any other community. Where we can have a laugh, a little play, some fun[p176].

Imagine a workplace where every individual is valued for what they bring to the diversity[p171] and creativity of the group, where everybody is allowed to have dignity and respect[p176].

Imagine a workplace where we build trust to start from an assumption of goodness, that we are all on the same side working with best intentions to

---

[8] *The Open Organization,* Whitehurst, https://www.redhat.com/en/explore/the-open-organization-book

achieve the same vision. When things go wrong, we look to the system first to understand how it is preventing people from achieving. When behaviours are bad, we look first to the system to see how it creates frustration and anger. Most often, good people are victims of poor systems.

> I get that the word "victim" is problematic. We need to be empathetic to the fact that people are NOT individually responsible for the system, nor can they change it.
>
> Only by a united desire from everybody to change does the system change. That can start from a guerrilla group locally and/or from the governors and executive. But for any individual, they're mostly highly constrained in what they can do, and heavily immersed in behaviours and culture that influence and affect them. They either develop negative behaviours out of frustration, or they come to genuinely believe they're doing the right thing. Blaming them for that achieves nothing.

"Hubbard's Razor"

Never attribute to malice or stupidity that which can be explained by moderately rational individuals following incentives in a complex system of interactions.

- Douglas W. Hubbard

Imagine a system where we don't set people up to fail by taking big bets on complex systems where nobody can possibly know the outcome with certainty. Imagine if we worked iteratively and incrementally, to mitigate risk, with a combination of agility and resilience to deal with all the world throws at us. And imagine if we accepted failure, in fact welcomed it as an asset of the organisation, a positive contribution of value from its opportunity to learn and improve.

Imagine if we constrained demand for work to levels that were sustainable and achievable; and accepted that results come when they come, at a time which is unknown until they arrive, and no sooner.

> Be impatient with actions and patient with results.
>
> - Naval Ravikant

This may seem idealistic, even naive about people. The reality is that there are dysfunctional behaviours that need to be dealt with; and even dysfunctional individuals who are unable to participate in the work community. But we should deal with these as individual issues, which is one of the purposes of people management. We should not design our entire system around stopping dysfunction. We shouldn't constrain and punish the group for the behaviour of a few, dragging everybody down to the lowest common denominator. We end up destroying freedom, suppressing diversity, and creating cultures that would be unacceptable anywhere else.

You can treat slaves, manual workers, industrial workers, and clerical workers ("transactional" workers) badly, and get higher productivity out of them through such abuse, but you cannot do that to knowledge workers. Knowledge work is invisible: the only way to get good work out of knowledge workers is to create a safe environment[p174] where they can flourish, and invite them to be part of the work[p212].

We soon find that what is essential treatment for knowledge workers, also gets better results from everyone else.

Even the most psychopathic executives should realise that the path to an optimum organisation is through the restoration of humanity[p160] and the creation of a healthy open culture.

> Rules should almost never be enforced, in the coercive sense. If every rule is there for a good reason, and if employees are motivated toward the success of the enterprise, then they should want to follow the rules.
>
> - Mark Schwartz

This does not mean that all behaviours are acceptable at work. In the same way that we socially moderate behaviour in the community, we should also moderate at work: anything that is socially unacceptable, or illegal.

In particular, we should expose behaviours at work which are covertly driven by unhealthy beliefs such as racism[p170]. As well as making the workplace healthier this will also make society healthier, since many people who harbour damaging beliefs spend most of their working day completely unchallenged in the current models, making them feel validated.

For the purposes of this book, I define "damaging" as contrary to who we want to be as an organisational entity. In a democracy, we decide that by majority consensus. In other systems, we submit to a power group. I subscribe to Laloux's model of social advance[p228], and I encourage you to work in organisations that do too. If you work (or live) in lower-level power-driven cultures, then what is seen as damaging will be different, and will be decided by a minority. In fact, the values of this book may well be seen as harmful.

We are animals, not thinking machines. We have primal needs as much as intellectual ones - colloquially, we have "lizard brains" [p237]. If people can be their whole authentic self at work, and exist in an environment of psychological safety, then they will be productive, collaborative, and contented. If people work for an organisation that they can believe in and feel safe in, then their productivity goes up greatly. This is well documented: for example, see Google's data-driven research in Project Aristotle[9]. This safety and sense of self will also have the effect of shaping the culture and then the vision of the organisation.

This has the broader social benefit of creating more ethical and moral organisations that represent the better principles of the society in which they function. Social consensus on principles is always moving. Organisations are obligated to track and reflect the principles of their stakeholders.

This is clearly not the case at the moment: good, normal people somehow twist their ethics to work for organisations which are acting in the interest only of their shareholders, creating a negative social impact. I'm going to guess this applies to many of the people reading this who work in private enterprise, who get pressured - and incented - into compromising ethics. What tax does your employing organisation pay? I've been subject to the cognitive capture of corporate culture. You come to believe it's right. That doesn't make it right.

When I worked for an American corporation, we were taught to hate our competitor as "the Borg". It turns out the Borg was a more ethical company, and many of the best people from my employer ended up working there. Meanwhile, our CEO went to prison for 12 years.

These work ideas have roots which go back decades, including kaizen, Lean, chaos theory, postmodernism, feminism, safety culture, and Agile. They draw from the work of Ohno, Deming, Rother, Goldratt, Wilbur,

---

[9] https://rework.withgoogle.com/print/guides/5721312655835136/

Laloux, Kahneman, Taleb, Drucker, Reinertsen, Snowden, Seddon, Owen, Hamel, Denning, and countless others.

> I'm painfully aware of how white and male that group of "well-known names" is: all men and almost all white men. The champions of these better ways are not diverse: they are the only voices that could get heard. Women like Donella Meadows or Mary Parker Follett are not amplified. It's slowly improving now, e.g. Amy Edmondson, but you still couldn't drop only her surname in this list and have many people know who she is.

These ways of thinking are not hypothetical. Pioneering organisations all around the world are demonstrating how they make work better, faster, safer, and happier.[10]

Beneath the movement in philosophy of work, there is a deeper and more profound shift going on in society, where for centuries truth has become separated from beauty and goodness, led by Western culture and the Enlightenment. That is to say, science has become separated from ethics and art. The workplaces that we work in today are primarily driven by science and truth, with insufficient influence from ethics and aesthetics.

The world is gradually returning to a reunification of these three "transcendentals": truth, beauty, and goodness. Postmodernism is not my favourite thing, but it is a step in this direction. So too are corporate responsibility, diversity[p171], ESG[p238], and stakeholder capitalism[p239]. As we focus on bringing more of our self to work, we must also focus on making that workplace more authentic and whole, more open: where we move from an obsession with shareholder value - the Friedman idea which is under serious attack in the economic world as we speak - moving

---

[10] Hat tip to Jon Smart's "better value, sooner, safer, happier" which became an excellent book *Sooner Safer Happier*.

from that obsession with value to a focus on values plural; and ensuring that the values of our workplace incorporate truth, goodness, and beauty in equal measure.

> The first Enlightenment perspective breaks complex systems down into discrete parts in order to understand them. A second Enlightenment perspective favours holism, 'joining up', connection and the systemic view. These are not alternatives but complementary views: the ideal is 'holism with focus'... the shift from fragmentation to wholeness is also about meaning. Without some conception of wholeness, fragmentation leads to meaninglessness. Story is a powerful way of making wholes from disparate parts and thus a strong form of sense-making (guiding action) in a complex world.
>
> - International Futures Forum[11]

Values and principles are not static, although they change slowly. I'm 62. My principles are not the same as they were when I was 22 or 42, although there are of course similarities. If one's principles don't change with increasing - dare I say it - wisdom, it's usually when they are founded on irrational superstitions. So too in society. Values and principles change over time, except when impeded by belief systems that are not willing to re-examine their principles in the light of new wisdom. Management should be rational in its willingness to examine new information and advance what we think (the word "scientific" has been spoiled in the context of Management, but that's what I mean). At the same time - if we are to be holistic - we must test that new thinking in the light of what society currently believes to be beautiful and good, to help decide what we accept and what we don't. Raw data is not enough.

---

[11] https://www.internationalfuturesforum.com/second-enlightenment

Part One: Exposition

As part of our transition to open ways of working, we all should reconsider our addiction to models of how we want to work, the way we look to them as easy answers.

Look at the misuse of the "Spotify model[12]", an idea that spread within the IT sector in the twenty-teens. Two very clever videos made with the then-new Doodly graphical tool, and suddenly everybody thinks "If we do the Spotify way, we will be Agile (p223)". No, not at all. Spotify the company weren't yet doing that - Henrik Knyberg was very clear about that in the videos[13]. It was an idealised view of what they could be. Even if they *had* been like that, it would have been a snapshot of a moment in time, because all good organisations are continually improving. And yet consultants made a full-time living going up and down the country promoting "the Spotify Model" as The Answer to Agile, a magic formula for success.

So too with Scaled Agile Framework[14] (SAFe®), Scrum[15], Theory of Constraints[16] (ToC), and Toyota Kata[17], and dozens of new pretenders. They depict ideal models or patterns not seen in their perfect form anywhere, yet their champions evangelise them passionately, even aggressively, leading to endless debates between the sandal and the gourd[18].

> Some of the proponents are downright fundamentalist. I, Rob, have had my moments with the ToCkers, the Katarati, the Scrum pack, the

---

[12] https://www.atlassian.com/agile/agile-at-scale/spotify
[13] https://youtu.be/4GK1NDTWbkY
[14] https://www.scaledagileframework.com/
[15] https://www.scrum.org/resources/what-is-scrum
[16] https://en.wikipedia.org/wiki/Theory_of_constraints
[17] https://en.wikipedia.org/wiki/Toyota_Kata
[18] This is a reference to Monty Python's *Life of Brian*, a movie rich in insights into the human condition.

XPdeists, and the Holy Writ of SAFe. I am turning model-atheist. "Both of us reject many models, I simply reject one more than you do."

This is true for models everywhere. My examples above are from IT, manufacturing, and management. The same can be said for economic models such as Marxism, Keynesian, or Friedmanism. Or political models like Communism, Republicanism, or Democratic Socialism. It is not a question of which is best, but how we can leave the debate behind, and rise above it.

It is not that they are the wrong models, but that models are the wrong approach entirely when we use them as templates for our organisations. They are aspirational ideals, not blueprints. Reality will always look different to the ideal model.

> Not more knowing (theories, frameworks, processes), but more compassion, more understanding, more "looking as" rather than looking at.
>
> - Michael K Spayd

I get asked about whether I base my work on Lean or ToC, waterfall or Agile, Scrum or Kanban, cybernetics or something-or-other, Freud or Jung (well, almost) .... The answer is I don't care.

I use elements of OpenSpace, Lean, ToC, Scrum, Kanban, Kaizen, Sociocracy, and who knows what else, as it suits the situation. Anything based on reason is fair game - which excludes some models, including much postmodernist thinking, any religion, and psycho-quackery like Myers-Briggs. Or Dianetics, which somebody seriously brought up on LinkedIn (I think it is the only time I ever deleted a comment). Critical thinking is essential to discern which-bits-of-what are useful to carry along, and which to reject.

I refer at times to Cynefin [p246] because it is a widely recognised sense-making framework [p246], useful in a VUCA world [p245], but truth be told I don't use Cynefin much in practice, as I don't use any abstractions except as background knowledge. I like Spiral Dynamics[19] and Laloux's "Teal" (obviously: the authors' brand is Teal Unicorn [p257]), for the stories they tell to illuminate the world, not because I think they are gospel truth or templates. I've seen harm done by people so immersed in theory that they've lost sight of reality. It turns to precious posturing pontification[20].

Not to go all mystic, but we must let go of the perfectionism around which model to use, the intellectual fastidiousness. It matters less than we think. Models are all a simplification that always fail to capture the colour, richness, and unexpectedness of human culture and behaviour. They dehumanise. The models are so divorced from reality in specific practical work situations that they only offer a light from one direction. If one model occasionally offers a wildly better level of illumination, then I pay more attention, but mostly they're all pretty dim. We need a bunch of them to see what we are doing. The looking matters more than the lights.

My work is very focused on practical actions in context. I may explain why I do something by citing theory when people want a rationale. I might refer to an "authority" to show I am not making it up. But I resist platonicity: I don't care about the theory, only what works. Work isn't about being theoretically correct. It is about finding what is possible to get the desired result. [No, that's not saying the end justifies the means. We should advance within our values].

---

[19] https://en.wikipedia.org/wiki/Spiral_Dynamics
[20] https://tealunicorn.com/philosophy-of-work/

> In theory there is no difference between theory and practice, while in practice there is.
>
> - Benjamin Brewster

I get caught out with ambiguous or incorrect terminology, or loose thinking. If I'm sloppy it is because I don't care. All intellectual frameworks are just planks we use to keep us out of the mud. They're useful but they don't need to be polished to a shine. We have a higher purpose than the constructs themselves.

As we have discussed, work is human. It is as much about ethics and aesthetics as it is about science and intellectual abstract models. At Teal Unicorn, I work with the mind and the heart[21]. It is not only about what's correct, but also what is right and appealing.

As your thinking rises above, the specifics of frameworks and models fall away as operational noise, and we open up to more important things, like humanity and thriving.

> As I rise above the treeline and the clouds
> I look down hearing the sound of the things you said today.
>
> – Pink Floyd

That is not to say that the stories that these models tell don't have a place, but that place is as an aspiration, a far-off goal, a navigational star [p226]. They are not there as building plans.

Or perhaps the stories have a place as a lens, a way of seeing the world. This is certainly true of Frederic Laloux's book *Reinventing*

---

[21] https://tealunicorn.com/work-from-the-heart/

Organizations[22], in which he presented a colour spectrum model of advancing cultures (p228), where teal is the highest colour yet achieved in the world (blue and violet are predicted in the future). The word "teal" has entered popular usage as shorthand for aspirational culture. Teal is also used by some as a specific organisational model "Teal", based on how Laloux described it - yet another intellectual model (p231).

> It is reasonable to have perfection in our eye that we may always advance toward it, though we know it can never be reached.
>
> – Samuel Johnson

Somebody debated with me on LinkedIn about Teal, and how Laloux was wrong. They pointed me to a website[23] which attacks him analytically, intellectually, academically, on a number of levels. It deconstructs his book from a scientific, logical, rational point of view. I refuse to engage in the debate, because that is not what Teal is for and that is not how I use it. It is a tool to inspire humanity, not to construct formal operating models.

> Personally, I find that sort of intellectual self-indulgence unhelpful in considering the real world. I know value can come of it if somebody more patient than me sorts through all the debate for useful ideas. Which is exactly what Laloux did. He's much maligned for ripping off the ideas he popularised, but again that's missing the point. He popularised them in a way that everyone else had failed to do. They are just jealous. I know I am. I wish I had written it.

---

[22] https://www.reinventingorganizations.com/
[23] https://social-labs.org/is-teal-the-new-black/

Philosophy is an intellectual exercise that isn't pretty to watch, especially in the context of work, which is about real-world results, not who has the biggest swinging intellect.

I listen to Dave Snowden now and then, because somehow out of the blizzard of abstraction that he produces, Cynefin turns out to be useful. There's a reason it is so well known. But I tune out of the stag roaring when the philosophers get together. I'll give the thread a quick scan to harvest what I can use practically in improving people's lives, then move on.

I'm sure philosophical discussion is important, in that the theoretical considerations do yield fruit from time to time. I try to track them, but I do soon wear out. Since they're all approximations of reality, any one will do. Some will do better, for sure, but a common understanding is very important in practical application, and right now the common understanding of complexity is with Cynefin.

Will we know a practical and useful "truth" when we see the results of an experiment? Yes. What real truth is, is for the philosophers. Work, like politics, is the art of the possible.

Philosophy of work is important, like testing science on animals is, but it is not something I want to watch, for similar reasons. Mostly because it seems to be done by men, and they produce a lot of aggression doing it, trying to establish dominance.

My work at Teal Unicorn comes from the heart more than the head. I am finding what works at a human level more than a mechanistic one.

I, Rob, find I can't deal with abstraction as much as I could. That may be chemo-fog (one of the after-effects of chemotherapy) but I suspect it is

> just age. I'm focused on going to the level of the practitioners I meet in the field, who couldn't care less about the theory. I'm heavily influenced by what Dr Vu is doing in Vietnam. What works. So my writing is less likely to be consistent or "correct".
>
> By applying the whole range of Human Systems Adaptability ideas, I am unlocking work in extraordinary ways. I've not felt the need for detailed analysis. I'm finding abstraction unhelpful.
>
> Meanwhile, I tell human stories from the heart mixed with all the familiar concepts of the better ways and together we raise companies up. People cry.
>
> This is my new direction, partly to play to my own strengths and weaknesses, but mostly because I see that Teal, resilience, agility.... none of these are analytical concepts, they're not amenable to abstract models. Something like Cynefin is illuminating, it opens doors to new ways of thinking, but I think it is as wrong, as overly simplistic, as any model.
>
> I'm dancing with the systems, trying to understand at a holistic human level what works. Just as the laws of physics aren't useful when actually sailing a boat, nor chemistry when trying to heal a patient, I don't find any of the models much use at the coalface of organisations.
>
> This rising above models is a new direction for me. I like to think I sniff the wind quite well, so I'm hoping it is a new direction for society too.

Another problem with such analytical thinking about work is that it treats organisations as machines, or even treats the individuals within them as machines that can be modified by psychological interventions and shaped to fit standard job descriptions. An extreme case is organisational behaviour management (OBM). While I am willing to believe that OBM works, that its psychological manipulations have a measurable effect on people's behaviour, for me that is beside the point. It is not a healthy way to think of your colleagues. I find the language OBM uses repellent, chilling. You are not training animals or tuning machines. You are dealing with fellow humans, colleagues. Leaving behind coldly analytic, dehumanised modes of management is what Teal is all about.

In the same vein, you can't reduce people to numbers. Measuring people is often worse than useless, it is damaging. The future of work is about the reunification(p231) of the transcendentals (science, aesthetics, and ethics) to return to total humanity.

The safety sector agrees - safety as in occupational safety, in aviation, medicine, mining, construction etc. Safety thinking(p191) is moving away from systems that modify behaviour, towards approaches to engage and understand people. This is connected to our general thinking about better ways of working, and it is influential on that thinking. We learn to embrace failure, to not punish it, to create transparency and learning. More of that later.

More broadly, companies don't get to treat people like shit any more. The social contract is near collapse: trust and loyalty are lost in most workplaces. These urgently need to be restored in our organisations. Hence there is a lot of attention on Environmental, Social and Governance (ESG)(p238) issues. Related to that, Gary Hamel and Michele Zanini's book *Humanocracy*[24] is a bellwether (a sign, an indicator of where we are going). Society is moving towards more humanity at work. It is not turning us into snowflakes, it is not a sign of weakness. It is making better people doing better work. Work should feel good. We should be

---

[24] https://www.humanocracy.com/

able to talk about <u>love</u> at work, to open our hearts as well as our minds. I'm proud to be "woke".

Psychological safety[p174] is finally getting a lot of attention. Even the most brutal managers might finally grasp that knowledge workers can't be productive when they're afraid: high value work is impossible in fight-or-flight mode: that lizard brain takes over. The whip - fear in all forms - no longer works. Firing[p205] is violence; those who remain see it, and deep in their lizard brain they remember what happened. You can't go around "shooting" staff and expect the remaining ones to be relaxed and happy. As we restore humanity to work, we rebuild trust, which opens up work.

Not before time either. The younger generations were not raised with an expectation of servitude. They won't put up with your crap.

Which brings us to the final issue with our conventional deterministic analytical ways of thinking about work: they don't work as well as you think they work, because they don't take account of complexity[p241]. Complex adaptive systems[p243] are VUCA [p245] (volatile, uncertain, complicated, and ambiguous). They do the unexpected; we never have a complete picture of the system or how it works; we have imperfect information: and we never know what the system will do in response to stimuli or over time. The only work that can be codified in a simple model is that which is defined and repeatable, and that only happens in highly bounded linear flows[p183], where the simplistic deterministic approximation is close enough. It takes a lot of energy to create these bounded flows - the classic example is a factory production line constrained by metal and concrete and rules.

Those simple flows all exist within a wider value network[p183] of co-creation, where direction becomes at least confused if not meaningless. Only at a local level - zoomed in - do we get approximately linear flows. What's more, those linear flows could potentially collapse out of the simple state (that Cynefin[p246] calls "clear") at any time if the bounds fail. When they do it is often catastrophic: search "rolling mill accident" on YouTube. As we open out to a wider view, we need ways of thinking and working in unbounded systems.

The world is always VUCA, always complex. Cynefin's Clear and Complicated situations are local phenomena when you zoom in, transitory bubbles of low entropy, achieved by artificial constraints bounding them. So, designing an operating model that doesn't deal with VUCA is a fragile approach. It is vulnerable to losing its bounds.

> The future is always unknowable. The future is never realised because change, paradoxically, is constant. The future is happening now. It is contingent on the past and, just like history, it never ends
>
> - Bob Geldof

This is a foundation for my objection to many thinking models or tools for work. For example, I dislike the feel of the Theory of Constraints[25] which to me is deterministic, mechanistic, logical. It fails the humanity test and it fails in its ability to deal with complex systems[26].

---

[25] https://en.wikipedia.org/wiki/Theory_of_constraints
[26] Its proponents will emphatically insist otherwise but I'm unconvinced

Or methods like Lean Six Sigma, where we gather statistical data to analyse work performance. In most contexts outside of factories, the assumptions are false: that the system flow is stable, that work is predictable, that we repeat the same transaction, that we can observe accurate metrics. Most work isn't like that. We require a certain number of repeated iterations to get statistically meaningful data. In how many contexts outside mass manufacturing do we do something the same way multiple times without anything changing? Seldom - either because we changed, the work changed, or the world changed.

Or take project management's critical path analysis. Anyone who can predict the future accurately enough to determine critical path on a Gantt chart should be worshipped. In fact, the whole of conventional project management is an edifice of lies, or perhaps, to be more charitable, theatre. Nobody knows what is going to happen in the future: what the end state of a project will be, when it will arrive, or what value will be realised. And yet we do this funny little planning dance to produce business cases and project plans, just so we can have some money because we created the illusion for those giving us the money that we know what is going to happen.

This last example of project timelines is important because it highlights that not only do we not know exactly what is going on; the future is unknown as well. We will come back to that.

> The only way it is all going to go according to plan is if you don't learn anything.
>
> - Kent Beck

"But my model/methodology works", they all cry. It may or may not. Correlation does not imply causation[27]. What's more, any intervention has the potential to have a positive effect, simply because people are examining their work[28] and cooperating to think about improving it, regardless of the methodology. They also want to justify the time and money spent on the intervention. You could use astrology as your model and get that effect.

Combine that with confirmation bias[29] - that champions of a methodology only report its successes - and anything can be seen to work. A variation of this is asking the chief executive whether the multi-million-dollar project they committed to for transforming the organisation was successful. Funnily enough, it always is.

My experience at Teal Unicorn is that application of better ways of thinking[p221] and working[p159] and managing - what I am calling Open Management[p195] - *invariably* works. There is clearly a causality, which one can see and understand.

Of course, my experience will be riddled with confirmation bias. Also, our clients are self-selecting: we don't sell, they come to us.

Let's ignore that, and make a deeper point: it is not about any way being better than the models. It is about rising above them *all* to look at why we do this, what is our purpose, and how we optimise to that. All the models become instruments in our cause, not an end in themselves. Our endless debates - tribal wars - over them become trivial.

---

[27] https://www.tylervigen.com/spurious-correlations
[28] The Hawthorne Effect
[29] https://en.wikipedia.org/wiki/Confirmation_bias

To summarise so far: idealised models don't serve us well as a pattern to build to, because:

- They depict an ideal never achieved. They are there to inspire, not provide a design.

- We would never get there anyway. Life is too random, and humans are imperfect.

- Most models are too mechanistic and clinical. They don't embrace the fact that they are about people.

- Most are static, deterministic models that don't take account of VUCA.

- They don't work as well as they seem to, due to confirmation bias.

As we will see, a higher cause makes all these better ways of working - all of Human Systems Adaptability(p159) - be secondary concerns, operational considerations in pursuit of our goals. We rise above all models. We can and should engage any number of ideas about work to help make it better, not make a cult of any one model. What matters is why; what matters is what we *do* with the models to become more open: to embrace humanity, transparency, and flexibility - to be immersed in who we are, where we are, and where we can go.

The classic Talcott-Parsons model of an 'integrated' organisation imposing its will on the world no longer applies. Rather, an 'organisation' is now a dynamic pattern of relationships between its own members and between them and an ever-changing world of competing loyalties and different value systems. It is a human system, a 'human being'. Albrow calls this an 'integrity' – an organisational form that maintains a moral purpose over time.

- International Futures Forum

Every organisation(p219) is a complex adaptive system(p243) that behaves rather like a living organism. Just like organisms, every organisation is unique: every one has a distinctive shape and nature that it arrives at from its initial makeup and its lifetime journey. Most of the factors involved in that journey are random, in terms of which factors were present and at what times they arrived. Which means that the nature of the organisation is not only unpredictable but also hard to control.

An organisation is not unconscious of this growth, since it is of course made up of humans. It is like an organism where every single cell is a consciously thinking being. So the analogy of an organism is not perfect. In fact, the organisation is in far greater control of its destiny than an organism - it has awareness.

> Maybe an organisation is even capable of self-evolution. I tell people off for using the word "evolution", especially when referring explicitly to the Darwinian natural selection model, when talking about an organisation changing itself. I object because natural selection is about the death of many organisms acting as a filter so that only the most suited to the environment survive long enough to reproduce. Natural evolution is not about one organism changing in its lifetime, it's about the death of many.
>
> When one says a single organisation "evolves", either the mechanism is different to natural selection and one is mis-using the word, or organisations are capable of consciously self-evolving their parts by selection, by reproducing some parts and killing others. I'm not sure which.

The point is that an organisation is constantly growing and changing in a way that certainly doesn't match some idealised template, and is absolutely guaranteed never to end up at that ideal state, because what happens is essentially random across a vast number of factors in a system that is too complicated to model.

> Learn to fix the system instead of fixing symptoms.
>
> - Niels Pflaeging

Let's stop using the ways of thinking as models. I don't use Laloux's concept of Teal as a design pattern for an organisation. I use it as a navigational aid[(p226)] to set direction, while the client and I try to influence the growth and development of the organisation. None of us have a great deal of control over that growth and "evolution", and one certainly can't predict where it will go. But unlike an organism, in an organisation we do have *some* level of influence. Donella (Dana) Meadows gave us the 12 points of intervention[30] for a complex system. We know we can do this, we know there are points at which we can influence the shape and direction. That influence is not on a passive machine or an unaware organism; it is an influence on a group of people. So we need to give those people a vision, a purpose, a narrative, a common cause to believe in; and a desire to be something better than they are now, to be open to change. That is precisely what books like Laloux's do, or the Spotify videos. They motivate people and give them a vision[(p227)] of who we might all like to be in the future.

> Simple, clear purpose and principles give rise to complex and intelligent behavior. Complex rules and regulations give rise to simple and stupid behavior.
>
> - Dee Hock

---

[30] http://donellameadows.org/archives/leverage-points-places-to-intervene-in-a-system/

The time is now. The world is falling out of seventy years of relative peace and stability. The COVID pandemic was the shock that woke everyone up from our complacency, but more factors will continue to make the world increasingly VUCA(p245): the rise of fascism; the rise of China; the ongoing technology explosion; falling poverty[31]; and of course runaway climate change. When I talk about surviving and thriving[32] in a VUCA world, I remind clients that we have very little control over *what* or *where* we will be, but - because we are human - we can all have much greater influence over **who** we will be, individually and as a group entity.

> If you want to build a ship, don't drum up the men to gather wood, divide the work, and give orders. Instead, teach them to yearn for the vast and endless sea.
>
> - Antoine de Saint-Exupéry

This is why I put so much emphasis on better ways of *thinking*(p221): on social change, on higher ideals; on the reunification of truth, beauty, and goodness.

Among the multiple causes of a VUCA world, the primary one, probably driving all the others, is the accelerating rate of progress in technology, especially in three domains: digital, biological, and materials. The biggest impact of this is sociological; society can't adapt to the new physical environment as fast as that environment changes. New technologies are disrupting all our social structures and behaviours, from government and politics to education and reading. Nobody agrees the codes of behaviour in new contexts like the internet, yet. Regulation emerges only in response

---

[31] If the planet is struggling now to support about one-and-a-half billion middle class, wait until there are four or five billion consumers.
[32] https://tealunicorn.com/st-happens

to problems once they become unbearable. And so on – you know the story.

Work must deal with this VUCA world. One progression in thinking, that is stumbling along behind this technological curve, is the advance that we see in how we manage that technology. Over decades or centuries, we have advanced up through stages (you can see this in multiple domains such as agriculture, railways, medicine, or IT).

The first stage is thinking about "Things": stuff, objects, the components. Then the domain grows or nature's progressively to thinking about:

- Practices: processes, rules, behaviours, wrapped around the Things.

- People: culture, teams, leadership. Who is doing the Practices.

- Systems: networks, emergence, complexity. Systems are made up of People, Practices, and Things, but we start thinking of them as an entity in their own right.

- Values: ethics, humanity, inclusion. These guide our approach to the rest, and lead us to principles and vision. The less we predict and control our systems, the more we need them.

Each of those advancing stages further encapsulates the ones before it. It looks more widely, enlarging the context of our thinking.

Within those advances in thinking to deal with VUCA, let's look specifically at our understanding of complexity. In the past, we were able to use simple linear models of reality. We said that we could define what we were going to do for a defined result; then execute; then measure how close we came to the defined result. The assumption here is that reality won't have changed much from when we define what we are going to do until when we finish doing it. In most domains, that is no longer true except for very short timeframes. Conventional project management - with its timeframes measured in quarters and years - has been called "delivering last year's requirements". It may have worked in the past but less so now.

There is a deeper assumption that also does not work anymore: that we can move from one stable state through an episode of change to another stable state. There are no stable states in most work systems anymore. Change *is* the state - it is persistent[p248]. Our processes change all the time, our software, and our knowledge. People come and go. The environment is in flux.

Treating the world as predictable was always an approximation. It worked when the pace of change was low. The target didn't move in the time it took to get there. Now our targets leap around like mad things. We often talk about navigational stars to guide us, but this is a misleading analogy. We pick a "north star" because it doesn't move much. All stars move slowly and predictably. Unlike the analogy, our "stars" in the modern world are more like fireflies. You look away for a moment and your target isn't there anymore.

The world never was stable. Life blindsides you. But conventionally, we would treat that as unforeseeable, the unexpected, surprising, an act of god. We would treat it as exceptional. It is not. It is normal for random things to happen – the world is random. The myth of predictability was only ever a mental model. Now it is becoming impossible to ignore the reality. We must adjust to expecting the unexpected, the black swan. We must act on the assumption that we don't know what the world is going to be. The future is disordered, foggy, random.

Look back to when we focused on understanding the world as systems near the end of the last millennium. We finally developed some rigour in understanding that those systems are complex, in a strict mathematical sense of the word, built around the new chaos theory. This leads to awareness of some basic principles:

- We can never know the whole of a system.

- We can never model or predict what it will do.
    - There is no function relating the inputs to the outputs.
    - The same input can result in a different output on a different day.
    - Success and failure can happen the same way.

- We cannot foresee what will happen when we make a change.

- There are emergent behaviours we cannot foresee. Some of them we cannot explain.

- The system responds to its environment. It may not be alive, but it acts as if it is.

- Everybody sees the system differently; we all have a different model in our head.

If we truly understand these principles, then they radically change how we think. If we tightly constrain the system within bounds and keep it simple, then a simple linear model can be used, such as a network diagram, process flow, or value stream map. But again, it is only a model, and it was always an approximation – the myth of the simple system. Not only is the future murky, but so is the present. It is not in the control we think it is.

I believe defining where you are going and when you will get there is not a profitable use of resources. Nobody knows - nobody *can* know. We can talk about the probabilities of future possibilities, but we have no way to test those assertions: we only test the future once. Probability tells you what will happen on average across many possible futures, but we only get one future, so probability tells us nothing. Almost everybody has trouble grasping this concept because it hurts so much to let go of the security blanket of having probability forecasts. Say it to yourself again: we know nothing about the future.

We know from experience that our extrapolated projections are often wildly off in hindsight. Actually, we plan the future in order to give us some comfort that we know where we are going, when we never do. It's theatre, and hence mostly waste. Planning has a small value as a thinking exercise, but mostly we wildly over-invest in trying to be psychic.

The language of "bets" is useful here. Every plan for the future is in fact a bet, and the bigger the plan the bigger the bet, with the bigger the potential losses or gains. Decision-makers should always be aware that they are gambling every time they talk about the future.

What matters are having values[p162] and principles, and our vision[p227] of *who* we want to be, that we use to guide us. We must aspire to be better people, and to understand well what better means. That is Teal Unicorn's slogan: "Make work better: better results, better lives, and better society" [p258]. I firmly believe that, in a better society where people are leading better lives at work, we will achieve better results for the goals of the organisation.

We can say the purpose of an organisation is to be better together than we are apart. It is in the name: corporation, company, society, alliance, organisation. They all speak to people gathering together in a single body, open to each other. That is nearly the right definition, it just needs a bit more. Read on...

There have been other attempts to define the purpose of an organisation[p219] of course. Peter Drucker said the purpose is to "create" a customer, which works best for business and has less relevance for government or not-for-profit (NFP)[33]. Setting the customer as our purpose has served us well but it is no longer enough.

Milton Friedman's toxic "doctrine" is that "The Social Responsibility of Business is to Increase Its Profits", which of course only has any meaning for a commercial corporation, and is actively destructive for NFPs and government entities.

Eliyahu Goldratt said the same thing in the much-lauded book *The Goal*[34], which is the basis of Theory of Constraints: "the goal is to make money" - another reason I don't much like ToC[35].

> No business is known to apply "profit maximization" to its planning or to its decisions on capital investment or pricing. The theories and concepts that govern the actual behavior of firms are theories of the cost of capital, of market optimization, and of the long-range cost gains (the "learning curve") from maximizing the volume of production rather than from maximizing profitability.
>
> - Peter Drucker

There is no doubt that the movement characterised as the Great Resignation will settle back to many people snuggling back into the corporate yoke of work as life. In the USA it's extra-padded with health insurance, but everywhere it's enforced by mortgages.

---

[33] Yes yes, Drucker was far more nuanced than that. But the simplistic view is what people take and run with.
[34] https://en.wikipedia.org/wiki/The_Goal_(novel)
[35] Yes yes, Goldratt backpedalled on the Friedmanism later, but the damage is done: the Goal is cited constantly.

The machine wants you productive, and the fruits of that productivity will go elsewhere. A widely shared metric is that wages purchasing power hasn't moved since 1979, despite productivity doubling. Somebody got all that wealth and it's not us. What's the harm of putting shareholders first? This is the harm:

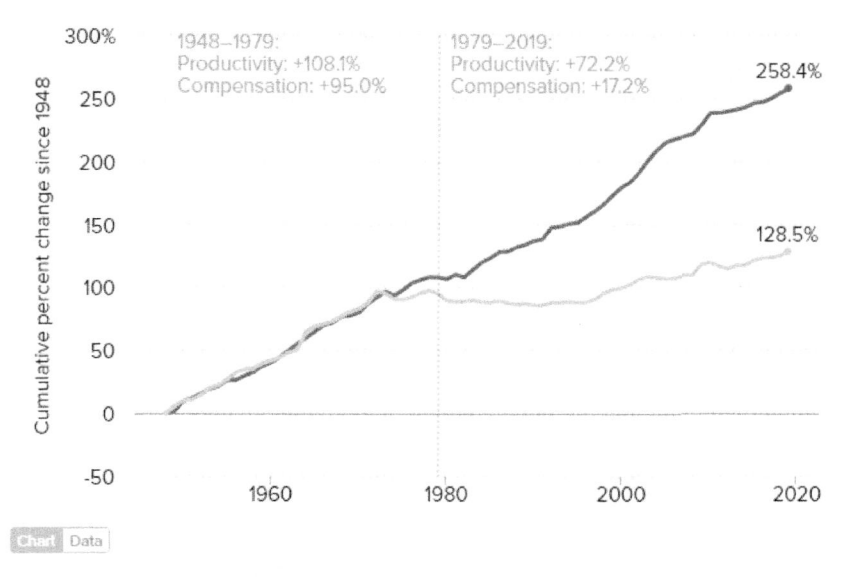

Productivity growth and hourly compensation growth, 1948–2019

1948–1979:
Productivity: +108.1%
Compensation: +95.0%

1979–2019:
Productivity: +72.2%
Compensation: +17.2%

Productivity: 258.4%
Compensation: 128.5%

Notes: Data are for compensation (wages and benefits) of production/nonsupervisory workers in the private sector and net productivity of the total economy. "Net productivity" is the growth of output of goods and services less depreciation per hour worked.

Source: EPI analysis of unpublished Total Economy Productivity data from Bureau of Labor Statistics (BLS) Labor Productivity and Costs program, wage data from the BLS Current Employment Statistics, BLS Employment Cost Trends, BLS Consumer Price Index, and Bureau of Economic Analysis National Income and Product Accounts

Updated from Figure A in *Raising America's Pay: Why It's Our Central Economic Policy Challenge* (Bivens et al. 2014)

Economic Policy Institute

Friedmanism[37] (I like to call it "Greedmanism") has been one of the most damaging beliefs of the last half century. It has brought us "greed is

---

[36] https://www.epi.org/productivity-pay-gap/

good"[38], several global financial meltdowns, environmental destruction, the obscene enrichment of a small number of oligarchs, and of course Trump as the reductio ad absurdum of the whole clusterfuck.

> I have watched videos of Friedman. I always get the impression of a smug, arrogant, heartless man. Many of our intellectual heroes aren't nice people, but that nature is evident in Friedman's model itself. It is hard to believe the cruelty is accidental: prisons for profit, wealth boom for the mega-rich, frozen wages, denial of basic care, elitist education, white privilege.

The world will be unwinding the damage of Friedmanism for decades to come. There is a strong movement to reject it[(p239)]: not to return to Adam Smith's[39] or Keynesian[40] flavours of capitalism, but to evolve to some higher form. There is of course a resistance: you can hear the howls of the old white men as they cling to everything they held dear at the end of last millennium which brought them so much privilege.

Individual nations have aspects of their work culture that need to be left behind as well, usually hangovers of obsolete belief systems. For example, Confucian unquestioning respect for seniority, Protestant workaholism, feudalism's slavery, colonial racism, caste systems, or militaristic admiration of force.

Growing adoption of a new way of thinking strikes resistance, of course, from the natural conservatives: religions, government, bosses, and not least of all the tech "bros" like Bezos, Zuck, and Musk, and their myriad

---

[37] https://en.wikipedia.org/wiki/Milton_Friedman
[38] https://www.youtube.com/watch?v=VVxYOQS6ggk
[39] https://en.wikipedia.org/wiki/Adam_Smith
[40] https://www.investopedia.com/terms/k/keynesianeconomics.asp

acolytes[41]. The political right wing is being driven deeper into extremist views globally, as it digs its heels in.

Am I too political? All work is political. Part of Open Work(p159) is to act with integrity(p162) and authenticity(p167). Another part is to create an inclusive(p172) workplace where people can be their whole selves(p164). The days when we were supposed to leave our politics at the door, to bite our tongues and get the job done, are gone. If you think about it, that is Friedmanism: "Never mind your ethics, turn that handle." The first edition of our book *The agile Manager (small a)* was impersonal and tried to be apolitical. This book isn't and doesn't.

> What is more, if you don't like my political views then you probably won't like these ways of thinking and working, because they are left wing, which always looks to the future - it is progressive where the right is regressive. These better ways are full of socialism, feminism, egalitarianism, freedom. It is more productive and more enjoyable.
>
> Am I too aggressive? Probably. I, Rob, am still learning to find and use inclusive empathetic ways to change minds. I have lost patience with the stale pale males of which I'm part. I see myself in them and reject it too hard. It is a personal failing. Cherry is much more temperate.

---

[41] They adopt business agility as a modern model, a pattern of work, but they choke on feminism, all forms of equality, and treating people with humanity:
https://www.cnbc.com/2021/04/28/amazon-to-hike-wages-for-over-500000-workers-to-up-to-3-an-hour.html
https://observer.com/2020/07/elon-musk-grimes-twitter-transphobia-pronouns-suck/
https://www.theguardian.com/technology/2017/jul/05/tesla-sexual-harassment-discrimination-engineer-fired
https://www.elle.com/culture/celebrities/a19746346/mark-zuckerberg-testifying-congress-facesmash-facebook/
https://www.theguardian.com/technology/2020/dec/27/facebook-to-close-controversial-irish-holding-companies
https://www.washingtonpost.com/technology/2020/06/25/tesla-plant-firings/
https://www.forbes.com/sites/brettonputter/2019/01/16/what-you-can-learn-from-the-facebook-culture-crisis/?sh=44ad39f64197

Bringing our whole self to work presents challenges in the workplace. What if someone's authentic self is antisocial? What if they want to convert everyone to their religion, or drive foreigners out, or put women back in the kitchen? Allowing authentic wholeness empowers diversity, which is the greatest source of innovation, and enhances the wellbeing and productivity of people. The problem is with a small number of people who are harmful to the diversity of the organisation. We need to find our own answers to that at work - I can't offer any neat solutions, other than to get better at weeding them out. I don't think it is acceptable any longer to put up with them as we might have done in the past. Nor is it acceptable for them to make an organisation their own enclave of antisocial ideology. Ask Activision Blizzard[42], a gaming software company, or My Pillow, an online marketing company[43]: ultimately it hurts the organisation, society won't stand for it.

We can be better. We can be so much better. Many voices are saying that today.

> There are all the activist shareholders which now represent some of the world's most powerful investors, who are demanding values over cold shareholder value[p240], from the organisations they invest in. They want to see progress on the Environmental, Social and Governance issues we mentioned above, a.k.a. "levelling up". Even Blackrock![44]
>
> There is the environmental movement, finally receiving popular support because of global warming (e.g. Greta Thunberg[45]).

---

[42] https://www.pcgamer.com/au/activision-blizzard-lawsuit-controversy-timeline-explained/
[43] https://www.newsweek.com/mike-lindell-admits-mypillow-cant-get-back-65m-revenue-lost-due-trump-ties-1580966
[44] https://www.blackrock.com/corporate/investor-relations/blackrock-client-letter
[45] https://en.wikipedia.org/wiki/Greta_Thunberg

There are the fresh waves of demand for women's rights (#MeToo[46]), racial equality (BLM[47]), social equity (the 99%[48]) and ecological action (Extinction Rebellion[49]).

And the Great Resignation[50], demanding a better deal for employees.

Taking account of all these forces, opening up to them, is known as stakeholder_capitalism[p239] a.k.a. stakeholder value (as opposed to *shareholder* capitalism - back to Friedmanism again). It builds on Hamel's "better together" purpose for an organisation. The stakeholders are a broad constituency, including employees, governors, customers, neighbours, owners, partners, suppliers, regulators, government, society, and ultimately the planet.

> ...companies with one goal in mind - to maximise human contribution.
>
> - Gary Hamel, Michele Zanini

Drawing on the ideas of stakeholder capitalism, my definition is:

the purpose of the organisation is to be better together, to bring greater value for all the entities it is networked with, all the way out to society and the environment we live in.

This is what Laloux talks about as Teal; this is what Clare Graves and Ken Wilbur and others talk about with Spiral Dynamics[51] and Integral

---

[46] https://en.wikipedia.org/wiki/Me_Too_movement
[47] https://blacklivesmatter.com/
[48] https://en.wikipedia.org/wiki/We_are_the_99%25
[49] https://en.wikipedia.org/wiki/Extinction_Rebellion
[50] I wrote more here
https://www.linkedin.com/feed/update/urn:li:activity:6870823847973785600/

Part One: Exposition

Theory[52]; this is what so many philosophers talk about with all the different models for social evolution[(p227)], which speak about some kind of a phase change happening around about now, where we currently are as a society. The International Futures Forum calls it a second Enlightenment[53] - I don't think that's an exaggeration. Even the hippies with the transition from the Age of Pisces to the Age of Aquarius were calling out something that they were part of.

```
New Ways of Thinking

            Game A      Game B
            First tier  Second tier
            Integral/Spiral
            Laloux         Teal

            Theory X    Theory Y
            Alpha       Beta
            Value       Values
              ♓         ♒  Aquarius
            Science
Spirit      Art         Wholeness
            Ethics
            Humanity
                                    v3
```

This diagram is in colour – a rainbow from red to purple. The original is at tealunicorn.com/nwot

---

[51] https://en.wikipedia.org/wiki/Spiral_Dynamics
[52] https://en.wikipedia.org/wiki/Integral_theory_(Ken_Wilber)
[53] https://www.internationalfuturesforum.com/second-enlightenment

This wave has been happening for a century, as we can see in the rise of democracy, human rights, liberalism, social welfare, the United Nations, global free trade, the food revolution, feminism, gay rights, gender identity, and general inclusivity. We see it in the setbacks to apartheid (in the USA and South Africa especially), and blows to fascism/totalitarianism (Germany, Spain, Italy, Japan, Iraq, Iran, Cambodia, Uganda, Chile…). Let us also not forget the amazing rise of prosperity across the planet[54]. And the explosion of science: more than half of all scientists who have *ever* been are working now. And of course, there is wildly advancing technology and its greatest gift, the internet, which has interconnected knowledge in ways undreamed of. The impact of the internet has led to its ultimate achievement (so far): the development of two hundred vaccines against COVID-19 in a crazily short period of time, just over a year.

The world has had a tough few years (I write in 2021) with the stain of Trumpist fascism across cultures everywhere, the puffed-up autocrats like Modi, Bolsonaro, and Johnson feeling empowered. And of course, a pandemic, though it is a mild one compared to viruses we know could come.

Longer term, we face daunting challenges across wide ranges, from post-truth delusion to climate change, overfishing to under-educating, Communism to Fascism, religion to racism.

Let's stay positive and take the macro view. The world gets better, society gets better. The United Nations' seventeen Sustainable Development Goals is a handy reference to current social expectations for that improvement. I dream that the 21st Century will continue the ascent of humanity, that we will see some of the following opening up: universal

---

[54] https://www.gapminder.org/videos/200-years-that-changed-the-world/

basic income[55], greater racial equality, the prevention of global warming, the elimination of absolute poverty, universal access to knowledge, protection of resources, the end of religion as a political force, peak population[56], fall of Communism and Fascism, holistic environmentalism, reunification of truth, beauty, and goodness[p231], and wonders we can't conceive of now.

All of this should inform how we think about work. We can make it better. We can liberate employees, embrace inclusive[p172] diversity[p171], maximise fluidity[p188], and treat all stakeholders with love[p177] and respect[p176].

This is the transition I spoke of above, the shift from conventional scientific management[p198] to open management[p195]. These ways of thinking, the social shift, are the philosophical foundations of the shift in work. It is not coming out of thin air.

We can treat employees better. Work to live, don't live to work. The work ethic in many countries is that work comes before all else. The philosopher Andrew Taggart calls this "total work" which undermines the whole point of existence. People who live a richer life than that bring their diversity and energy to work: it is in the organisation's interest to encourage better lives.

Besides, we need the rest. You can work a manual labourer to death and get productivity most of the way, but knowledge workers quickly fatigue. Most of us reading this are only good for 2-6 hours of high productivity work a day.

The elephant in the room is the shift in power: when you're a knowledge worker, organisations and their management need you more than you

---

[55] https://en.wikipedia.org/wiki/Universal_basic_income
[56] https://www.gapminder.org/topics/population-forecasts/

need them. Incidentally, managers are knowledge workers too. Just sayin'.

Nobody has the right to pressure[p203] or punish[p204] anyone else, least of all in the belief that it is for their own good. People may *choose* to work hard on something. That's not the same as having pressure imposed on you at work. Nobody has the right to abuse others in the name of work. Nobody should be treating workers like objects to be shaped or processed. We get to shape ourselves, voluntarily, in our own way, as free adults. Letting people determine their own work is basic human rights, not to mention love and respect.

A business culture has been built up glorifying overwork, a burnout machismo. This is organisational gaslighting. If you accept this work pressure, that's a victim mentality. If you don't know and agree why you are working hard, and if you are not consciously opting in, and if you aren't satisfied by it, then that's abuse. Even when you opt in, examine your beliefs closely to ensure you have not been indoctrinated against your own interests.

In the extreme, when people work to death (karoshi) or worse still, they commit suicide, management should be accountable, as France Télécom found out[57].

It is fascinating watching the incredulity on LinkedIn when somebody suggests that staff should be able to duck away for an important family event. "Impossible! You can't run a factory/shop like that!" Absolutely you can. People do.

---

[57] https://www.theguardian.com/world/2019/dec/20/former-france-telecom-bosses-jailed-over-workplace-bullying

Part One: Exposition

The drive to efficiency in business, to deliver maximum money to owners (Friedmanism), has led to understaffed teams and rich owners. Hamel and Zanini's book *Humanocracy* covers this well.

> The 21st Century is a different game with different rules... The pursuit of efficiency was once a laudable goal, but being effective in today's world is less a question of optimizing for a known (and relatively stable) set of variables than responsiveness to a constantly shifting environment. Adaptability, not efficiency, must become our central competence.
>
> - Gen. Stanley McChrystal

But efficient systems are fragile, as shown by the collapse of global supply chains in 2020. In this VUCA world, our top priority has to be adaptability[p187] not efficiency, and that requires the agility[p223] and resilience[p192] that slack capacity gives us. Tom Demarco explained this in the book *Slack* twenty years ago. And Drucker and Deming said it even earlier. With slack capacity in a team, and proper empowerment to allow self-organisation, they can figure out rostering amongst themselves as grownups so they can get to those family events.

It doesn't matter if it is a shop or a factory or a hospital: once you stop staffing for 100% (or 110%) people utilisation (i.e. stop staffing for minimum cost), and start staffing for resilience and agility, acknowledging the unpredictable world, then you will build slack capacity. If you start treating employees like grownups, and empower them to self-organise, then if somebody needs to duck out for a couple of hours it is possible. If somebody is below full performance, dealing with a personal issue, the others can carry them without an unfair burden.

And if managers start serving instead of commanding, inspiring instead of coercing, then people will want to get the job done. They can take ownership of the decision-making process[p215]. They are not slaves. They are people with complicated lives. Be human. Work to live not live to work. We should not subjugate people to work.

There is a flip side to this. There is an enormous productivity potential to be unlocked in most work systems. We may not need more people if we can fix the bureaucratic constipation of the existing system, open it up. *Humanocracy* covers that too.

> The only constant in life is change   - Heraclitus

 But don't let the trite management mantra of "work smarter not harder" get organisations off the hook for the fact that there are enormous surpluses being skimmed off systems around the world by a few people. We can afford to have more people and higher pay in business if owners take less profits and executives less grotesque salaries. We can have the same in government if corporations and the rich paid their fair share of tax. We're overworked because we are being overworked to profit others. More capacity is essential to better work.

As well as this shift in social expectations, there is a second foundational shift in the world. This is the increasing rate of change. Change is now the condition, the state we live in, not something that happens episodically. We can no longer plan and work assuming the world will be the same tomorrow. As we said, the world is VUCA. To survive in such a world, the essential capability is adaptability[p187] - openness to change.

To encompass this shift in work, I use the terms Open Work and Open Management, inspired by Dan Mezick's Open Leadership Network[58], of which I am a member. (I don't say "open manager", because I already wrote *The agile Manager*, so let's not confuse things. This is open

---

[58] https://openleadershipnetwork.com/

management for agile managers. Maybe the next version of my book will be *The Open Manager*).

The term "open" may go back to the second International Symposium on Organization Transformation in 1984, run by Harrison Owen, where he started the Open Space[59] technique, but I'm not clear when he first coined the term. The term "open source" originated in 1998. We know who came up with it[60] but not what inspired her. In both cases, using the word "open" is a product of the social cultural evolution to liberate, to make transparent, to invite, to include.

I think "open" is going to be a big word in future discussions of work - as big as "agile" is now. We are opening up the organisation like a flower: letting light and air in, making room to move and grow, exposing the workings, inviting others in, welcoming, creating possibilities, allowing pollination, letting the value out, letting us thrive.

"Open Work" is an umbrella concept, encompassing many ideas. If I try to organise them, I find three main themes: Open Work is about Human Systems Adaptability[p159] (my own term again).

Open human culture, with integrity, transparency, liberation, inclusiveness, and collaboration.

Open work systems that flow freely, focused on customer value, with fluidity of work, of teams, of organisation.

Open adaptable behaviours that explore with curiosity, embracing whatever comes, responding to a changing world, planning dynamically.

---

[59] Properly called OpenSpace Technology, where "technology" means it is a tool, not a reference to any software or equipment. https://openspaceworld.org/wp2/what-is/
[60] Christine Peterson, at a strategy session held on February 3rd, 1998 in Palo Alto, California, that led to the Open Source Initiative, OSI.

Human Systems Adaptability means we set people free in free-moving systems to freely pursue value. These better ways of working overturn some beliefs and principles of the conventional workplace. It's not that we totally stop doing what we did and replace them. We move our priority - we value these things over those[61]:

From	To
Big bang: plan, describe, do	Agile: iterate, increment, experiment, explore
Organise around projects	Organise around products
Stick to the plan	Change the plan often. Try not to plan. Make decisions at the last responsible moment.
We know what will work	The only way to know is to try
Zero risk	Every risk is always possible
Failure is unacceptable.	Failure is normal. Failure is the path to success.
Mistakes are preventable. Human error is a root cause.	Mistakes are inevitable. Human error is a design constraint.

---

[61] Those who know IT Agile will recognise the format of its Manifesto.

Part One: Exposition

Accountability and punishment improve quality.	Punishment destroys learning.
Standardise roles.	Let the team distribute work, according to skills not roles.
Fix your weaknesses.	Build your strengths.
Maximise utilisation.	Maximise throughput.
Improve everywhere.	Focus on constraints.
Maximise work in progress.	Limit work in progress. Maximise throughout.
Secrecy and controlled access	Open and shared information
Short term incentives	Long term sustainability

...and many more.

> It is the system that governs behaviour... when the system changes, behaviour changes in tandem; and to change the system we have to change the way we think about management.
>
> - John Seddon

In order to work in better ways, to do Open Work, people need to be managed in better ways: Open Management. (We wrote more extensively about both in our companion book *The agile Manager*(p255). We summarise - and occasionally update – here in this book). It is hard to change the way you work if the system within which you work is unchanged. We can change within the old system by creating protected bubbles, opening a bit of white space around the new way, but not for long. If you still have the same old goals, policies, funding, processes, metrics, reporting, and incentives, nothing will permanently change. I see this as the most frequent reason for failure when organisations try to change the way they work: they fail to change the way they manage.

> Right now, your company has 21st century Internet enabled business processes, mid-20th century management processes, all built atop 19th century management principles.
>
> - Gary Hamel, Michele Zanini

To enable better ways of managing, the governance must change too, although not necessarily straight away. Again, we can do a lot within the old system, but we must hack the organisation to make it happen if it is not coming from the top. Make these changes to management within your sphere of influence, then see that it attracts others to your light. Eventually, the values, vision, policy, and direction set for the organisation need to change to enable managers to change. And they usually will, once the organisation learns about the better ways, has the internal proof points, and sees that they really are better: better results, better lives, better society.

This requires patience[p208]. No matter how fast the world moves, humans have a slower rate of change of behaviour. This tension is the cause of much harm when we force change too fast (e.g. my pet hate of big-bang restructuring).

> Maybe you are searching among the branches, for what only appears in the roots.
>
> - Rumi

The biggest shift in ways of management is from bosses to gardeners, from commanding to nurturing, from power to service, from Theory X to Theory Y. The term "Beta" is used, as in a shift from Alpha stereotypically-masculine command-and-control management to Beta[62] stereotypically-feminine servant management. While not all male managers will be comfortable with a 'feminine" label, part of the new ways of thinking is to move on from the gender models that cause that discomfort. You'll get used to it. It doesn't challenge our manhood.

This is Open Management. When managers are servant gardeners, they can increase our ability to get work done, instead of obstructing it. Alpha managers are as likely to prevent work as to accelerate it. So let's include better ways of managing as well as working and thinking, to take us towards better work.

---

[62] Dana Ardi framed the Alpha-Beta model of management in her book *The Fall of the Alphas*, in 2013

Related to this is an ethical[p166] shift. Business can no longer insist it has a different moral standard. It is no longer "just business". It's not ok to lie, or bully, or play dirty, or evade social accountability. It's not war. That kind of thinking rots society. At its mildest, we end up neck deep in bullshit[p168]. At its worst, eBay sends a bloody pig's head and live cockroaches to a critic[63]; the British Post Office lets people suicide or go to prison when they know they're innocent[64]; whistle-blowers have their lives destroyed; or labour organisers disappear.

We must aspire to a higher standard of behaviour. We open our management to bring out the best in people.

This isn't some naive kumbaya idealism. We do need to deal with human nature and expect bad behaviour[p170], and have people management in place to deal with it, but if we don't start from a position of trust and then adjust accordingly, we will never liberate work to achieve higher culture and higher performance.

Work needs to feel good: to do the right things, to get them right, and to have a good time doing it.

> While "losing control" is one of the biggest fears in management, "having control" is one of the biggest illusions.
>
> - Bjarte Bogsnes

As well as this change in behaviour, another shift in management is the structural changes, from rigidity to fluidity, from closed to Open, from bureaucracy to humanocracy, all summed up as Human Systems

---

[63] https://www.wired.com/story/ebay-employees-charged-cyberstalking-harassment-campaign/
[64] https://en.m.wikipedia.org/wiki/British_Post_Office_scandal

Adaptability. All the behaviours of Open Work should be reflected in Open Management.

> Strategy is a mental tapestry of changing intentions for harmonizing and focusing our efforts as a basis for realizing some aim or purpose in an unfolding and often unforeseen world of many bewildering events and many contending interests.
>
> - John R Boyd

I distinguish between three forms of management:

- **Work management** including planning, delivery, quality, projects, and functional (finance, legal, facilities...)

- **Personnel management**, including recruiting, development, pastoral care, specialist areas, performance management, and coaching

- **Executive management**, including ownership, figureheads, vision, principles, policy, and strategy.

I also recognise a fourth form of "management", which is a coach. They have some responsibility for and toward people, but the word "management" doesn't sit well with them. Whether you include them as another management group or not is up to you. I'm still exploring that.

These forms of management are often merged into one job, one person. That isn't optimal. There is real benefit in separating them out, or at least not expecting someone to be able to do them all.

Work management and personnel management are separate but intertwined, often described as a matrix, or a dual helix. Executive management sits under both, which all sit *under* those doing the work and creating value: be servant managers[p210]; flip the hierarchy[p211].

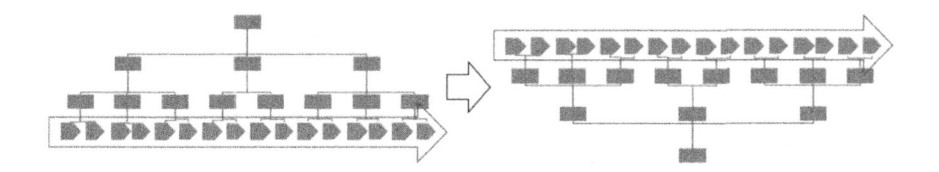

I don't use the word "leader" for management (or try not to). Leadership[p219] can happen in any role: it is a behaviour, not a role.

The Executive is the representative of the Governors, acting according to their direction to operate the organisation. The Executive Managers are the source of culture, and of change. The fish rots from the head; a badly-behaving boss will ruin their domain within a year or two. Good executive management leads their organisation upward, but it takes longer. A tree is slow to grow and quick to chop down.

> Consciously or unconsciously, leaders put in place organizational structures, practices, and cultures that make sense to them, that correspond to their way of dealing with the world.
>
> This means that an organization cannot evolve beyond its leadership's stage of development.
>
> - Frederic Laloux

In most companies, all three kinds of management need to be reshaped, and maybe over time reduced, but not eliminated. As part of this advance to humanistic Open Work, there are often calls for the elimination of management. This is a mistake, throwing out the baby with the bathwater. In the same way that attacks on Friedmanism are not a rejection of capitalism, or calls to defund the police are not calling for the abolition of the police but rather a refocusing of their purpose, I think the same thing should happen to management. There is a function to be performed within organisations that does the organising. My definition of management is organising the people and resources of the organisation to achieve outcomes set by the organisation. It is certainly possible that a group can manage the work itself with no managers. My simulation game The Message[65] teaches exactly this. So too do the furniture companies owned by Cherry and her family - hundreds work with a few leading hands and a couple of managers. Which indicates that we can certainly descale management. We could conceivably get to the point where we have "no managers", and the activities are dispersed as skills across the teams. But eliminating it entirely may not be the optimal solution, as some specialisation and centralisation - management as a service - is often more effective (and efficient, though that should never be our reason) than complete dispersal.

More than this, distinct management performs a useful function. Managers observe and think. Managers step back from the work, to see the bigger picture. Managers connect dots. They are the sense-makers, and the source of much innovation. Taylorism has poisoned the concept of management for many people. We need to get over it, and see that the right kind of management is an essential part of a healthy organisation. It's not management that people are opposed to per-se; it's a certain kind of management that they have experienced.

These better ways of managing overturn some conventional ideas around management, just as better ways did earlier in the book when thinking about work. Again, we want to shift our values:

---

[65] https://tealunicorn.com/message

From	To
Answers come from above.	Answers come from the work.
Organised team	Self-organising(p180) team
Being tough is essential.	Be nice, and authentic(p167). Vulnerability takes courage.
Command and control	Servant(p210) gardener
You have to measure it to manage it.	Measurement(p199) is an aid.
Optimise for efficiency.	Optimise for adaptability.
Slack is waste.	Slack is optimal.
Centralize, elevate, and limit authority.	Distribute, disperse, and share authority(p212).
Need to know basis[66]	Open transparency
Ruthlessness	Decency and generosity of spirit

---

[66] No kidding: I know an organisation where the staff newsletter is called *Need To Know*. Ouch.

Management practices

In our book, *The agile Manager (small a)*, I identify eight[67] activities that characterise an <u>a</u>gile manager, a manager working in these better ways:

Attracting

Managers act as an attractor, a magnet bringing resources and people together around a stream of work. We are inclusive, we build diversity. We throw the net wide, bringing in as much as we can to get results. We gather and orchestrate resources to help people. We recruit when good people are available, not when we have a vacancy to fill.

Nurturing

A manager is a gardener: we provide the conditions and the inputs for people to flourish and a work system to emerge. We encourage constant learning in people, and improvement in systems. We provide resources, guidance, care, and feedback (positive and negative).

> The question you should be asking: Not "What can you provide?"– but "What can you provide others in order for them to be effective?"
>
> - David Cancel

Liberating

Modern managers flip the conventional hierarchy: we act as servants of the value work. We give staff the authority, capability, space, and resources to get the job done. We define the challenge not the solution. We open the work system up, remove impediments, get out of the way, and trust people to find the answers and do their work. We lean back, make room, hold space. Let the people doing the work design the work.

---

[67] Actually, six in the book. We have added two more since.

We deal with controls and reporting so that those doing the work don't have to. "Get out of the way" doesn't mean "Go away". Managers should be intimately involved with the work, at the gemba(p213) (the place where work is done), while making sure not to be an impediment or constraint to the flow. Helping with some of the work is great.

> Strategy gets set at the top. Power trickles down. Big leaders appoint little leaders. Individuals compete for promotion. Compensation correlates with rank. Tasks are assigned. Managers assess performance. Rules tightly circumscribe discretion.... That constitutes the operating system for virtually every large-scale organization on the planet.
>
> - Gary Hamel, Michele Zanini

Motivating

Managers give people the vision, goals, incentives, and most of all the feeling of engagement(p207) to help us all want to achieve our goals. People are invited to work, and given the authority to do so. We provide intellectual challenge and emotional excitement. We give people a reason and a desire to do the work, and we build confidence. We restore humanity to work.

Navigating

Until we reach full self-organisation, managers will always have more familiarity with the broader directions of the organisation than their teams. Collectively, management will determine these directions, in collaboration with everyone. Even if managers share this information perfectly, it is still their task to keep an eye on alignment with these directions. There are also times when decisions are still required of management, especially in fast-moving, high-risk, chaotic situations.

Exploring

We allow freedom, we look for better ways, we understand that diversity means discovery, we stimulate curiosity. We take intelligent risks, embrace failure as the path to success, welcome the unknown, and see chaos as opportunity. We look for innovation opportunities, through discussion and observation. The source of much work innovation is managers[68] - we have time to step outside the work and think about it.

Observing

Managers keep close to the work. We observe, monitor, and measure how it is going (all three of those: don't fixate on only the measurement[p199] - there is much we can't measure well). We analyse work and track trends. We provide fast feedback everywhere where it is needed, from the people doing the work to the governors, across all parts of the value network from customers to colleagues.

> You don't need a weatherman to know which way the wind blows.
>
> - Bob Dylan

Representing

In this outward-facing activity, managers stand for their people at times. We speak for them, advocate for them, explain, report on, listen for, and protect them. Until we reach Teal nirvana, management will still collectively determine directions and actions at the macro level for the organisation.

---

[68] *Gemba Kaizen: A Commonsense Approach to a Continuous Improvement Strategy*, Second Edition, Masaaki Imai (2012). A good read but beware it contains some outdated concepts.

Open Management unlocks Open Work, and Open Work will unlock productivity, which is held back right now by the demotivation and cynicism induced by Friedmanism, combined with the restraints of bureaucracy. Hamel and Zanini convince us in *Humanocracy* that the productivity bonus will be immense when we escape both.

Teal Unicorn has a model for dealing with a complex, volatile world, which I call *S&T Happens - Surviving and Thriving*[69]. It brings together everything I have discussed. The five aspects of this are:

- Better ways of working, for agility and resilience: "Open Work" (p159).

- Better ways of managing to enable change in work: "Open Management" (p195).

- Better ways of planning, or more precisely, not planning (p184) [70].

- Advancing safely towards new ways[71].

- Capitalising on turbulence and failure[72] - opening to opportunity.

That is getting outside the scope of this book, but it is included to show how these ideas all come together. For more details, refer to our website, and of course *The agile Manager (small a)* (p255).

To advance, we must be open to possibilities. Only the present and past are known, (and only uncertainly, and ambiguously), not the future. Sonja Blignaut expressed this well[73]:

---

[69] https://tealunicorn.com/st-happens/
[70] https://tealunicorn.com/st-with-new-ways-of-planning/
[71] https://tealunicorn.com/new-ways-to-advance-our-capability/
[72] https://tealunicorn.com/thriving-on-adversity-and-opportunity/

> When we understand the dispositional state of a system, we can also recognize Kairos moments, opportune times when the system is poised for change. Cynefin is about embracing the here and now; we learn from the past, but we don't rely on it to predict a future; we are evolving into a future, but we are not aiming at an idealized future state. We search for the evolutionary potential in the present, and when Kairos moments arise, we take them... Cynefin methods are based on finding the evolutionary potential in the present, setting a broad future direction, and moving towards 'adjacent possibles.'

I wrote down the ideas that Dr Cherry Vu coaches in Vietnam, which lead to the amazing results you can read about in the stories in this book. Cherry's message is simple:

- You can't make people do good work. You need them to want to. You can only invite, motivate, and inspire, then get out of the way and enable.

- Respect, empower, and trust your staff. People want to do their best.

- Be better people. Aspire to Teal. Reflect on your own behaviours and their effect, the messages they send.

- Make work better: improving results, and even more on improving the working lives of your staff.

- Embrace failure. Make it an asset not a cost.

- Fix the system, not the individual.

---

[73] *Cynefin: weaving sense-making into the fabric of our world*, Snowden et al

- Ask questions, don't tell. The answers are within your staff. Explore together.

- Don't try too much. Step by step. Experiment locally. Experiment with anything in our book *The agile Manager*, especially:

    - Team goals not individual. Work as a team.
    - Collaborative rituals within and across teams.
    - Change how managers manage. Servant management.
    - Visualise work.
    - Skills not roles – fluidity of work. Let people self-assess as shu-ha-ri[74], with peer review.
    - Self-organising teams – fluidity of structure
    - Cross-functional teams
    - Work with staff to simplify work systems. What do they need?
    - Map the value stream(s). Simplify flow.
    - Open the books, be transparent about finances.
    - Let staff work out how to apportion pay, first the bonuses, later the salary.
    - Pay people to leave. Work harder at recruiting the right people.

- There is no formula. Stop asking consultants. Every group is different.

- You don't need to believe or trust me. Try it.

That's it. No one method: Cherry teaches Lean, Agile, Kanban, ToC, Kaizen, Toyota Kata, whatever... It doesn't matter. What matters is Human Systems Adaptability[(P159)], especially the human bit.

---

[74] As defined by Martin Fowler https://martinfowler.com/bliki/ShuHaRi.html

Let's grow our little bubbles of better ways one team at a time, and then one organisation at a time, as a thousand points of light for better work in future. It is the duty of the agile manager to foster and protect those bubbles, and to advance these better ways across the organisation.

That's Better Work. That is the gist of it. I have described how work can be better by being more open. And I have made my core point that work can't get better until management does. Better management is open management.

Next you can read our case studies. There are many more stories we will capture when we can. We have no hidden failures, no stories we don't want to tell. This isn't selective, it is representative.

Can it work elsewhere? I was asked: what is different in Vietnam? My answer: not much as far as I can see. There are superficial cultural differences, but all over the world people are people. All the human patterns are the same. We discuss this at length in a recent article in the Business Agility Institute's journal, *Emergence*.[75] It is reproduced in Part Two, below.

When we have (a) chief executive access and commitment, with a willingness to self-reflect and change, and (b) an autonomous unit of business that can change freely; then there seems to be no constraint on rapidly opening up better work: better results and better lives.

It has worked in SMEs: real estate, small manufacturers, online retail, wholesale distribution, schools ... And in large legacy corporations: manufacturing and banking. So I don't see why it won't work for you.

---

[75] https://businessagility.institute/emergence

Now it is up to you to open your mind and your management to better ways. Join our community[p10], share what you learn like our clients do (Part Two), and learn[p251] what you feel the need to learn.

That's the end of Part One, the Exposition of my ideas. The rest of this book is elaboration on these ideas. The remainder is a series of notes to expand on the main text, not always a coherent flow.

Part Two that follows is the stories I have to tell: one fictional, and several case studies.

Part Three is the endnotes to this book: the elaborations which were refered to from Part One. They're readable as they stand as well, so keep going.

Part Two: EXPERIENCES

A collection of narratives sharing the actual experiences of the Authors and our Clients in exploration of Open Management

Image: Đỗ Cẩm Lai

Part Two

Storytelling is a force for good: stories communicate far more far faster than facts, theories, and diagrams.

> The most powerful story of all is the organisational narrative, the story we tell each other about who we are, where we came from, and who we want to be: the Origin Story that all communities crave to give themselves identity.
>
> Next are the legends, "tall tales and true", of past events and characters, that help preserve and transmit the culture.
>
> The third tier is anecdotes recounting recent experiences, as proof points within our organisation. Use these liberally, especially if you can get them told first-hand. They are more powerful than all the facts, numbers, and ideas you can cram into a slide deck.
>
> Fourth are stories from elsewhere, the experience of others, showing us WDGLL: What Does Good Look Like; or, equally, warning us of the pitfalls, the hard lessons learned.
>
> Finally, fifth, come the fictional stories to illustrate ideas. A picture may paint a thousand words, but a good story beats a dozen pictures.

Therefore, we include a number of stories here to make this book clearer. Some of you may be perplexed or frankly incredulous. That's ok, these ways of thinking flip many conventional ideas about work on their heads. Perhaps an example will help. The first story, "Narwhal Design" is fictional, but not hypothetical: it combines many of the experiences we have seen or heard about. You can download this story in pdf form[76] to share. It is reproduced from our book *The agile Manager (small a)*.

If you prefer our actual experiences in the field, skip to the Case Studies (p87).

---

[76] http://twohills.co.nz/public/A_short_extract_from_the_agile_Manager_v1.pdf

Narwhal Design, a tale of agility

Simon owned a costume jewellery manufacturer, Narwhal Design. He knew something was wrong with the company. Their competition was beating them out of the market with new designs and faster delivery. Everything he tried wasn't helping. So he brought in some advisors to help who a friend had recommended.

The first thing the advisors did was to walk around. Talking to those doing the work, they soon learned his designers were frustrated because Simon had to approve all of the designs personally, and, frankly, Simon didn't understand what customers wanted. One of the first changes made was to convince Simon to believe in his designers, and free them to approve their own designs as a team. The designers would be rewarded based on the success of their designs in the market, and the higher the sales the more likely that a designer would have their future designs chosen by their team.

Building on this example, the advisors convinced the management team to rip more approvals out of the workflows. They ran workshops with teams to challenge the controls, and everybody agreed to take a lot of unnecessary governance out in many places. Plenty of managers were relieved not to have to do rubber-stamp approvals that they had never understood anyway. The advisors were careful to review and beef up the risk management process to ensure that gates weren't being left wide open. Work freed up in many areas. A lot of workload came off managers and governors.

Managers started to be uncomfortable. Simon was always keen on reducing head-counts, and some of them were feeling extraneous. The advisors put them to work re-designing the reporting structures. Everywhere that line managers - or even worse, workers - had to do reporting work, the managers were to change the process so that a manager observed the work, noted the data, and wrote the reports themselves. This got managers out of their offices and further freed up the workflows. (It also exposed that more than half the reports served no useful function, or were redundant; suddenly managers want reporting to be efficient when they have to do it themselves.).

Digging deeper into that flow of work, it was discovered that the team building the prototype jewellery to test the designs weren't really talking to the designers at all. There was a strained relationship between them because of past frustrations: the designers are the higher-prestige team, and wouldn't accept feedback from the prototyping team if a design was hard to make. The prototypers had to figure out how to build a design, and were seen as having failed if a design was unbuildable or had problems in production. All communication happened through their managers, often escalated up to the common boss, Simon.

The advisors sat the two teams down face to face and led them to talk through the issues. They were asked to create better feedback and iteration between the design and prototype teams, to make sure that designs were practical. This was to happen directly, not through managers, and preferably by getting up and walking over there. The team managers also organised informal activities between the teams, a curry lunch every Thursday, where they could informally talk about anything they wanted as well.

The next step in the value stream was passing the prototype to the engineering team to set up the factory to make the jewellery at large scale, and then a production run. There were many delays in manufacturing and sometimes a design would not be produced fast enough to catch the season it was designed for, or to meet the customer's delivery expectations. It turned out that production runs would need to be set up two or three times, only to be cancelled part way when something more urgent came along, or when a design fault was discovered part way through the run, or one component hadn't arrived in sufficient quantity. Then the half-completed products and materials needed to be stored somewhere (where it was sometimes cannibalised to meet another shortage). This was news to Simon, and to everybody outside of the production factory. The factory had been managing the turmoil internally, presenting a brave face. They didn't want to show how bad the problems were: Simon wasn't good with bad news.

A lot had been invested in "increasing efficiency" in the factory. Production lines ran flat out, never pausing longer than they had to for a re-fit for a new product. Staff - including managers - were exhausted. The slightest hitch (and there were always some, due to design and materials problems) caused work to pile up everywhere. With such high utilisation in the factory, the work still moved slowly.

The advisors applied Lean methods to map the value streams. They analysed the flow of information, and quickly showed that production's chaos wasn't entirely of their own making, but also came from failures of communication and low-quality work elsewhere. These other areas thought the defects were trivial, but the impact of these small hiccups were catastrophic on a factory running flat out.

They analysed the flow of work of a design from initial idea all the way to delivery of product to the market, and the flow from materials to market of a single piece of jewellery. Although each department's workflow was well understood, nobody had ever tracked the timelines end to end.

This uncovered a big time-lag between prototype and production which had lain hidden to pretty much everybody except one clerk who did his job diligently managing the huge queue of work. And it showed that all the work to speed up the factory had actually only addressed a few percent of the total time of a value flow, and in fact slowed the over-all cycles down with all the chaos caused by them being flat out. It was making them worse.

The advisors coached the clerk and the factory managers to introduce a visual work management system, on the wall outside the clerk's office in a corridor where everybody could see it. Every new batch of work appeared on the wall as soon as a design was in prototyping. It flowed across the wall, with its status and problems shown in different colours. They had to expand the column for the backlog that the clerk was managing because nobody had realised quite how much there was.

A new gating technique was introduced, where work didn't start until it was 100% ready, with all materials onsite and a tested design. Materials were locked down on a palette dedicated to the job so they couldn't be cannibalised. If a job needed more material than fit on one palette, then it had to be split into smaller production runs. The job went up on the wall in a backlog of work ready to run. The senior managers agreed the priority of the runs for each day, and everybody had to agree to suspend a job part-finished. All the planning and decision making was done standing in the corridor around the planning wall. This kept meetings short.

Simon was upset that he was excluded from the advisors' whole improvement process. His advisors explained to him that it was better to let the people doing the work design the work without him in the room. He didn't like what he was hearing about reducing utilisation in the factory, and holding work until everything was ready to start. It sounded like backward steps to him. He wanted to know what was going on, but the advisors kept him at arm's length.

A crisis came six months into the changes, when Simon realised that the factory was working in new ways that he didn't understand, and the designs being produced were ones that he would never have chosen himself. The sales results were yet to be seen, and he was deeply uncomfortable about losing control of his company.

He became moody and critical of everything. He was deeply frustrated that he seemed to be losing control of his own company.

Then several things happened to change his views.

One of the largest projects which Simon's advisors had convinced him to do was to consolidate several small lunchrooms into a new larger area in an unused end of the warehouse, fitted out with a kitchen, good coffee, and nice new furniture. There was even a barbeque outside and some indoor plants! The senior managers also lost their own private lunchroom, which was a tough battle. Simon was brooding in the brand-new cafeteria one lunchtime - worried about its expense and the message it sent while the company was in trouble - when the background noise finally intruded on his thoughts. It dawned on him that all he could hear was laughter and chatter at energy levels that he had never heard in the company before. He looked around and saw tables with staff from all parts of the organisation sitting together in conversation.

Several days later, he went for a walk around the factory, as his advisors had coached him to do. He asked the foreman of the production line about a problem with a particularly complex piece of jewellery, and she said "Not to worry, we worked it all out over lunch with the design and prototype teams". Simon had resisted the new cafeteria, because he saw them as time-wasting spaces. He had kept the lunchrooms small and cramped to encourage people to get back to work, but here they were breaking down barriers, and having a good time doing it. Had he been wrong all along?

Where the factory joined the warehouse, there was another open area in the warehouse, and a new table tennis table had appeared. Nobody was using it at the time, but Simon scowled anyway. And where was all this free space in the warehouse coming from? It was a worry if buffer stocks of materials were being run down. And yet Simon knew throughput and profitability of the factory was up, with less stocks and apparently more spare time. Something didn't add up.

He was walking down the corridor outside the production clerk's office and saw several employees standing around the wall covered in work, in heated conversation, working out a production problem. Simon stopped to ask what the issue was, and made a call to help resolve the deadlock. Only after he walked away did he realise they were all low-level team leaders and – gasp – actual workers, and that it had been so easy to resolve because they were involved directly in the work and knew exactly what was going on. A similar problem had been an agenda item of his executive team meeting over and over again for weeks in the past.

When he got back to his desk, the initial sales figures had at last arrived for the latest round of designs, and it was clear from the numbers that one of the designers had a particular flair. Three of his designs were selling hot, higher than any previous design the company had produced. They were all designs that Simon would have rejected. He felt crushed. He had been holding back his own company.

Simon met with one of his advisors, Amalia, who had become something of a mentor to him. She had introduced him to the habit of walking meetings, so they set off on a stroll away from the factory. She sensed he was unhappy, and soon had him sharing his disappointment in himself.

Amalia explained that such a reaction was natural, and some of the self-criticism was valid. "But don't be hard on yourself, Simon. You built a successful company. The recent problems were a sign to you that what got you to here isn't going to work anymore. The world is changing too quickly. You can no longer keep up with design tastes as you once could. It was time to let go of that. Your customers want more variety and they want it faster. The old production methods that were so low cost can't keep up any more. The world is still scrambling to come up with these better ways of working and managing. They haven't been around long and are still evolving. You didn't cause any of that to happen. That is change in the environment. Our job is to increase your agility to deal with that new environment. You need these new ways, and you are already seeing the results, even if you still have plenty to improve. Look at it this way: you feel bad because things are getting better. That's silly. Celebrate with your staff. Throw a party."

So they did.

Case studies

Perhaps, instead of the hypothetical story above, you would prefer some case studies from actual clients of ours. (Or skip to an article summarising our work in Vietnam on page 145.) These case studies have been machine-translated from Vietnamese, then cleaned up for readability. I tried to leave them in the authentic voice of the clients as much as I could. My comments are in *italics*.

Vinh Duc: Self-organising through the J-curve to better performance (p89)

LOC: Reorganising everything to better ways of working (p105)

LINHPOHS: Precious time back through very human agile thinking (p119)

ERICK: Real and effective ways of managing and working (p129)

LamLuy: Working more efficiently, and happily (p135)

Check on our website[77] for more.

---

[77] https://tealunicorn.com/clients/

Vinh Duc: Self-organising

through the J-curve to better performance

It is hard to overstate just what an amazing case study that Vinh Duc Real is, so I want to preface the story told by Hằng with my (Rob) own reflections on the journey over more than a year.

Not only did Hằng completely reinvent the operating model for a real estate agency of 40 people, so that they were self-organising teams, completely fluid as to size, structure, and duration; but then when most of the staff realised what a dynamite model it was and decided to go off on their own to start a new agency, this didn't create any hostility or friction. Hằng supported them in doing so and maintained a business relationship, so that they continue to share clients and properties, to their mutual benefit. As a result, Hằng now operates with 5 staff, has reduced her office space and all her operating costs, and still gets the same revenue as she did with 40 and makes much more money than she used to. Everyone has three times higher income.

Consider just how advanced this example of management is – straight out of the best of contemporary management textbooks. Completely self-organising teams is the Agile that most organisations dream of. Growing staff until they fly free with their own business and then remaining collaborating with them is pure Green from the Laloux model – one step away from Teal. Hằng has made it work with courage and conviction, through the support and advice of Dr Vu.

Part Two: Vinh Duc

I'm Huỳnh Thúy Hằng (Sarah Huynh), CEO of Vinh Đức Real Estate Agency[78]. I founded this company four years ago.

We have 40 staff involved in arranging the sale of properties, as well as investing in land and houses, in Ho Chi Minh City, Vietnam.

Hằng came to our agile Manager training in Saigon several years ago, and keeps coming back for more. She brought along her managers, and she joined Cherry's weekly online coaching group. She and Cherry talk several times a week to coach and support her, but we are not consulting onsite: Hằng devises and implements her own solutions.

---

[78] https://bannhabinhthanh.vn/

Previously the sales staff were divided into teams: a fixed number of 5-8 people in a team with a team leader. When a team was organised that way, everyone functioned and interacted within a small scope under the supervision and support of the team leader. We found that organising teams this way caused bad workflow that hindered the development of individuals. People had to spend a lot of time reporting. Also, to do a sale, a team leader needs to support their team members in every transaction, as well as to pay attention to very small details such as punctuation, as well as the working attitude of everyone.

As well, experienced members who can independently sell had to still report and receive support from the team leader (for example, making contracts, etc.), that led to a lot of work for the leader, wasting the time and skills of every party involved, and left no time for improvement. When one member did not fit in the team, they were afraid to switch to another team although they thought it would be more suitable. The leader of the team was still active in sales themselves, which led to a conflict of interests among the members and the leader. Everyone was unhappy, tired. We rarely saw interaction, coordination, and information sharing with other team members. This lack led to ineffective results.

We decided to set the teams free. We took team leaders out so it was up to everyone to organise and manage themselves. People choose anyone that they can coordinate with to form a team naturally. It can be a group of 2 people, 3, 6-7 people, and also people who work independently but have a support team whenever they need it.

This was not as rash as it may sound. They had made smaller experiments first with one team to verify it was workable.

In the beginning, we still maintained the support of team leaders to support the members when needed. Later on, we formed an official support group, where everyone can come to them whenever they need.

The support team does not specify exactly who they will support: any worker can share with one or all three members of the official support group, as long as they feel safe and can best support his or her problem.

It is important to understand that this support group was made up of three experienced ex-team-managers – they were now servant managers. They provide specialist skills in contracts, administration processes, negotiation, and so on.

During the month after changing the way of working, the performance of the whole company dropped significantly because people were not familiar with the new way. The level of interaction decreased, the collegial spirit went down, people felt bewildered, and most of them wanted to go back to the old way, even though there was the agreement and consensus of 100% staff before starting. They had all agreed on the obstacles.

During that month, some people formed a team and worked well, some people had difficulty forming a team, most felt helpless and wanted to return to the old way and didn't accept change.

Beware the "J-curve" (see p189). It always happens on any change.

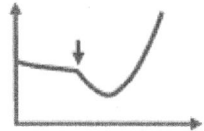

We then had a half-day company meeting, under the guidance of Rob and Cherry from Teal Unicorn, to help:

- identify the principles for the whole team to follow

- draw the value stream to find the reason why transactions fail, where are the bottlenecks, why performance drops

- decided some areas for improvements, an action plan for things that can change immediately and what needs to be done in the future

- decide what needs to be done to support and coach those people who are struggling with the new way

- establish trust between individuals.

We conducted a visioning exercise to create focus on company values. Some staff looked a bit mystified or cynical during the exercise, but later in the afternoon they came to realise its value. Cherry gave a motivational speech about why it was happening, how a J-curve was normal, and how collaboration was essential for them to now rise up.

Then we split the staff into three groups for 90 minutes to look at the value stream and what the blockers were; who was struggling and what support they needed; and what were the opportunities for immediate incremental improvement. Staff self-selected their group, so most were engaged.

We found the big problem was that people lacked trust to collaborate, share information, and help each other among staff. As well, people did not have adequate support from the company to timely guide them and remove obstacles in the process of working, leading to the performance of the whole company and the morale of people going down.

After discovering the problems and finding solutions, we had many successful transactions. Specifically, in the first 10 days of October, Vinh Đức successfully sold 9 properties. In 20 days, we sold more than the number of sales in September. All are the results of good collaboration between members. Even new staff who in 5 months hadn't sold any property were successful in selling houses.

Some people left initially, but we think that is because poor performance is made visible. Culturally, people are not accustomed to being exposed: in other organisations, many coast within the group. Then numbers became stable and morale was up.

Their success continued. Sales were not as high as they would like but the market was flatter than the previous year (this was still pre-COVID). This is one of the challenges with organisational change: it is never a controlled experiment, there are always multiple concurrent changes, some out of our control. Cause and effect is never provable – it is only ever a hunch. We must beware of confirmation bias.

An experienced manager shared:

"One of the great things about the new way of working is that even though you're still in the support group and have the role of a leader, you no longer have to do micro-management, so we have time to sell and still care about others. Staff no longer have to spend time reporting, but spend most of their time selling, cross-interacting, and diversifying with many staff that they used to hardly talk with before."

When I talk to people about what they think, I notice the changes are huge. Some staff were very harsh at the beginning and did not support the new way of working but now they think differently and are more active. People in the company are more creative, always looking for ways to improve their work, to help each other, the more experienced ones help the newcomers, the better salespeople cooperate with the less successful members. They often tell their friends about the company and how we operate, and everyone likes it.

Of course, it was not all rosy. They had challenges getting the demand balanced across the three people in the support team: everybody prefered to go to one. We coached them to hold a group workshop to design how support should work; and the three support staff worked out how to load balance amongst themselves.

Other challenges continued. Commission schemes are an endless source of debate, and are probably never optimal.

When approaching the perspectives, ideas, and methods from Teal Unicorn, I know what is right and what is good and how to get there. If I had not learned things from Rob and Cherry, if I hadn't been greatly encouraged and accompanied by Cherry, it would have taken so long or I would never have stopped to improve. I would never have thought about ways to set people free and to be better together.

Part Two: Vinh Duc

Thanks to her guidance and daily feedback to our work, we learned the stages of change and how to face it. I know and believe that I can do many things with the team to make them happy. I was fortunate to have the chance to attend Cherry's training courses to know about the right and beautiful things, so my mission is to help my people to be better, with sincere sharing about where we are going, why we are going that way. They will not be afraid to go along with me.

Our next step was to encourage the group to study each others' ways of working, to understand the different models emerging, and their pros and cons. Then a support function can hold this knowledge and coach the teams. Vinh Đức was to open a second office in the new year. This knowledge would be essential to allow them to scale quickly. But things changed ...

At Teal Unicorn, we never give answers or "design solutions" (although sometimes we offer suggestions). Nobody knows how this agency should work. Those best equipped to find out are those doing the work, through experiment and exploration and sharing. They continued to collaborate, and to adapt to changing people, demands, and conditions.

I realized that I was able to apply it partly because I brought all my managers and some key people to Cherry's training courses, so when I proposed an improvement, no leader left me. Initially, some group leaders were somewhat disappointed when their roles were removed, but thanks to the knowledge they obtained, they are aware of many things and still accompany me.

By now, the sales results of all team leaders are superior to the previous month. One of them got 5 successful transactions/month which was previously only seen in the sales teams, even though they are still in the support team.

Team leaders used to get commission on their team performance. Now they sold directly themselves to earn commission. This created conflicting incentives. We suggested to Hằng to pay them commission on the performance of the whole branch. This allows them to focus on supporting and coaching, and to work on management functions: sales, marketing, customers, finance, information, personnel, operations, risk, and assurance.

I am not alone, and happy to see that people are truly creating more value, no one has to drag anyone, seeing my people grow up day by day, just like I plant seeds and they become big trees. Now it is time to fertilise to get more sweet fruits.

Hằng has been with us from the beginning, has given us so much support, and is now a personal friend. We were so happy and relieved to see her company humming with strong managers emerging, as she was pregnant with her first child, and we did not want to see her stressed. We hoped she could step back with confidence and enjoy the new stage in her life.

Teal Unicorn awarded Hang "Best contribution to our community" in 2019.

Part Two: Vinh Duc

2021 update

Hằng and her baby are going great. So is her business. In 2021, Cherry gave us an update on Hằng, transcript translated here by Rob:

Cherry: WHEN YOU HAVE DREAMS, YOU WILL SEE THE WAY. One day this energetic young CEO emailed me:

I read your articles, hear you talk about agile management and agile enterprise, I see that's what I've been searching for so long. I wasn't happy where I worked in the past, nor am I satisfied with what I am doing now. It is not the working environment that I want, where everyone works effectively and happily. Can you help me?

Cherry: Since then, whatever training course Teal Unicorn has run, she joined and brought her team to learn too; she read the books I recommended to read; and did (most of) what I suggested she should do. She told us:

In me, I see the determination, persistence, curiosity, wanting to explore, wanting to assert myself. I desire to improve every day and most of all, I believe one day I will get what I want. After a year of training and coaching, I was able to master a lot of knowledge and skills and led my team to become a fully agile team, which means that I can respond quickly to change.

During the 6 month period applying an agile management method, the cost of the whole company decreased by more than 60%, everyone got better, they had more skills, and could take on many different jobs.

After 3 months of applying an agile sales method, previous problems such as conflicts of interest, bad cooperation in teams were completely eliminated. Everyone backs each other, working best to win together in every deal. Everyone in the company is happier, and everyone's income is better.

I realize that when you have a dream or a goal, the most important thing is to believe in yourself. People will tell you it is not possible, but when you connect with your dreams, nothing can stop you. Of course, you still need the right support, but if you don't believe in yourself, all support is meaningless.

Cherry: *And of course, old man Rob [it is a Vietnamese honorific, no comments please] and I are extremely happy, the gardener's happiness when we see the trees we work hard for. The people around me get better, their lives are better.*

Part Two: Vinh Duc

The rest of the story

Hằng said costs fell by 60%. How can that be? There is a final chapter to this story. In February 2021, we made a video in English of our success stories in Vietnam[79], and Hằng's was of course the first. Here's what Cherry says in the video:

The first case I want to talk about is the CEO of Vinh Đức, a real estate company. When we first met, they had more than 40 employees. They had a problem with the middle management and with the culture. There was too much competition - they paid employees individually. Before we met, every team had one team-lead, and they only worked within the team to exchange information. Also because they paid individuals and they didn't have a fixed salary or some monthly salary or anything like that, if you sold a house you could get a big commission, otherwise you got nothing. They had a management team and the leader of that team (Hằng) never worked with people. She actually only worked with team-leads. They also had a functional team for finance, legal etc who worked closely with leaders, and that's it. So you can imagine how the culture would be in real estate. What people sell is actually the information, but people didn't share information with each other because it is risky for them. When we started working with her, we saw the problem that the middle management – the team-leads – actually created a lot of constraints in the system. So we took out the team leads. We also created the supporting team: the supporting team is made up of some specialists who have more experience than the others.

That created work structures that went much faster and they got higher revenues and higher income. The staff worked like this: if you like someone for a particular deal you can work with them, they work loosely,

---

[79] https://www.youtube.com/watch?v=LNkrdm6zT6w

every single house has a different team, it depends on who will be best for the deal.

After that we said why do we need a functional [support] team, why don't they just join the team and create the end to end process, and that makes everything much faster.

Later on Hang also joined the team: the CEO is also one of the members of the team. She's no longer controlling anything.

But the biggest change and the biggest outcomes came later on, from the change of payment: when they changed the policy from paying individuals to paying the team, it was much different. The teams had been self-organised, but conflict of interest was still there because of the individual commission policies.

With no manager at all, the structure of the company no longer has hierarchies or anything like that, it is just flat. I am a fan of "Inviting leadership" and "open management" so I asked [Hang] that every single thing, every policy, every decision, you should put it on the table – don't do it yourself, stop making a decision. She stopped making decisions, put everything on the table, democracy.

People gradually learned more and more skills. Before that they had very limited skills, but now everyone can do each other's work. They have cross-functional teams, pay people based on skills, and all the teams are organized by skill, using shu-ha-ri. All the skills are in the group that are needed to finish the work, from the learner (Shu) to people who are good at work (Ha), to a master (Ri). So they divide people into shu-ha-ri level and they join teams so as to make sure that, for every single skill, they have one – at least one – who is good. That's based on self assessment and group evaluation.

Part Two: Vinh Duc

We created a learning organisation to make sure that every week they have at least two hours for learning, exchanging ideas, concepts, and understanding. Even though they don't have any roles or don't have any team-lead or promotion, they are happy because all of them are better, they have better skills, they have more experience, they have more income. Here's a result you can see:

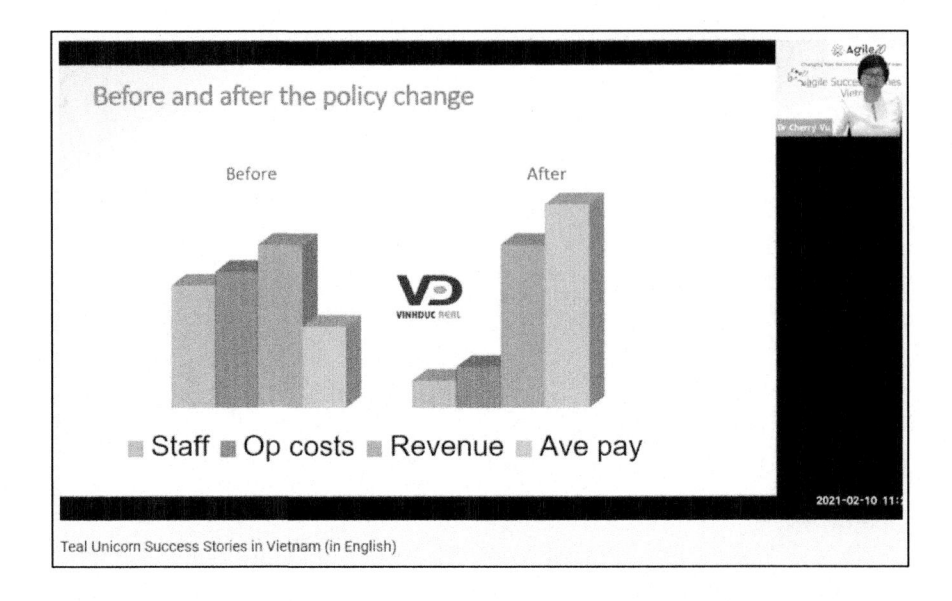

Before and after the policy change

Before | After

■ Staff ■ Op costs ■ Revenue ■ Ave pay

Teal Unicorn Success Stories in Vietnam (in English)

Before we changed the policy, they started from June 2019, and up to now you can see the difference. You can see that the number of the employees dropped a lot [*down to five!*] just because some key sales didn't like the new arrangement: they wanted to have a great sum of money rather than to share with others, so they left. [*An even bigger bunch of employees left to form several of their own companies to exploit this better way of working. Hang was initially concerned but Cherry coached her. She kept working with them, so they share properties and clients, and hence commissions*]. Operational costs also dropped a lot. Revenue is still the same [*a much smaller number of people made just as much money!! So that...*]. Average payment for employees increased hugely [*about triple*].

I'm very very proud of this case because of the outcome, and people are much happier, and they feel like every single day they are going to have fun.

More about Hằng

If you speak Vietnamese, and you are curious about the CEO Huỳnh Thúy Hằng[80] and what she does, we invite you to watch this Facebook video https://facebook.com/groups/353382871937665?view=permalink&id=678547746087841

This is video No. 3 in the series "Agile Thought Connected Community" by Tien Thuy Tran[81], one of our students who was so impressed by what her sisters in management were doing that she made the series of videos interviewing them. We love when this kind of initiative emerges from our tribe.

---

[80] https://www.facebook.com/PeChuot89
[81] https://www.facebook.com/groups/353382871937665/user/100009942062345

LOC: Reorganising
everything to better ways of working

I am Nguyễn Thị Nhường (Su Nguyen), Founder and CEO of LOC Group Fashion Joint Stock Company[82]

Su left university to start a research and production programme on rimless bras in February 2016, and officially launched her lingerie manufacturing business in July 2016 with Loc, her boyfriend, naming the company after him. She later went back to graduate from Ho Chi Minh City University of Medicine and Pharmacy as a doctor.

---

[82] http://www.facebook.com/dolotkhonggong

As the competition is as fierce as war, the elimination and "natural selection" are increasingly taking place on a broader scale requiring Vietnamese businesses to adapt to survive and thrive whether they like it or not.

From the beginning, LOC has asked questions and looked for answers: How to develop in the fashion industry that has this fierce competition? Fortunately, LOC found our partners Teal Unicorn who teach us and give lots of useful advice.

After participating in the training course "Becoming an agile manager" and a workshop "Applying better ways of working and managing" – simulating a business that has changed from an ineffective bulky business into an agile business – we applied these concepts to LOC's manufacturing practices. This is the story of LOC.

The workshop was our simulation game, Diggers[83], which Su has attended several times, as she learns something new each time. She brought a number of staff along to it.

The problems in the past:

The production division was not well organised: The cutting section was far from the sewing line, as well as the quality control (QC). It took a long time to transport from cutting to conveying, exchanging, returning and replacing wrongly cut goods. The QC department was away from the assembly. There were isolated working areas and poor information flow.

The QC department found many product errors, and lots of conflicts occurred. More product defects showed up even after delivery to customers.

---

[83] https://tealunicorn.com/diggers/

The warehouse took a lot of time to search for raw materials. Warehouse staff were not aware of the orders to be put into production, so they did not know in advance what materials to prepare. They often gave wrong or incorrect amounts of materials to the factory.

We did not track the amount of goods needed to produce an order, especially urgent orders, or goods with special details.

Percentage of errors, damaged, or mouldy products were high.

Productions which didn't have all sizes done remained in the warehouse for so long that it led to fading of color, poor quality, and the need to throw them away.

Information flow between different units was not good and clear, which led to confusion and slowing.

Some people in some sections had to do too much. As a result, there were bottlenecks in different places.

The whole organization was overloaded, busy but productivity was low.

The improvements LOC have made:

1. Rearranging the sewing factory

Relocating to a new location to have more space and more facilities. Every section is located at the same place.

All units were rearranged flowing in a Value Stream.

Units are separated by a dividing line on the floor: better information flow, people can see each other's work, better support for each other.

Renamed units according to their functions to show what they create.

Part Two: LOC

Described the work of a coordinator and a tailor-made model so that more qualified people work for more specialized jobs.

Rearranged raw materials (thread), dividing into 3 main areas: the most common thread colors, only for the sewing collection, the less used threads, stick lace with threads. Reduced time for searching for thread and comparing thread to lace.

Arranged bra padding types, colors, size of the pads, dividing cup sizes and their colors before cutting to reduce a lot of time in the process.

Gave each sewing worker a basket to put the items that were used during the day. The end-of-day unprocessed product will be put in a carton to continue working the next day. Personal belongings were stored in a shelf to avoid having too many objects around the production line causing confusion and difficulty to find items.

Put baskets on the production line divided into two categories of goods: urgent orders and normal orders, from which all members can see the product flow making it easy to control and very easy to find them.

Used different color baskets so the priority mode is clear for each different type of goods. All employees see the colors and they know which goods are prioritized then they can complete quickly and timely.

Introduced transparent plastic cards with a note inside showing product specifications to avoid paper loss during the movement on the production line, thus ensuring the right model and right number after completing.

Rearranged wire parts by specifying quantity and color sizes of each type of wire, eyelet, or hook. Reducing time to search for them and everyone can get the materials they need.

Contained materials that are waiting for assembly, assembling, or already finished products in plastic boxes with lids, and glue on clear information to reduce dirty, mouldy parts, and make them easy to find.

2. Reorganise the warehouse and its operations

Rearranged the warehouse of raw materials, controlling the amount of in and out and inventory.

Warehouse staff know in advance the amount of materials needed for upcoming orders and actively prepare enough quantities.

3. Improving wire cutting unit and QC

Checked the execution time at stages and then divided it into work groups to reduce errors and arrange work in cadence.

Rearranged the workflow to create a seamlessness between workplaces: sewing line –> QC –> putting pads. The cutting unit has changed the pattern to help it be done faster, easier to sew, less cropping. Reduced cutting time and saves more materials.

A week after changing, the productivity increased to 150% and all inventory in the QC department was resolved within 2 weeks.

4. Visualise workflow and information flow

Encourage all departments to make a kanban board so everyone can see the workflow.

Support each person, each department, to ensure people know each other's work and manage their work well.

Using pictures to visualise customer feedback so that everyone understands the value of their work

Organise every morning stand up meetings, list the tasks that everyone will do today and the priorities.

Top priority is the flow of information: after receiving the information, a coordinator will notify each department with a note of the latest information and place it in the most visible place.

Agree on common principles to ensure that everyone is aware of the change and correctly understand the change, which helps to avoid incomplete or incorrect information.

Develop models and specifications for each product category then provide information, catalogs and products to all divisions.

5. Creating a united environment throughout the company

Organising monthly birthday parties for employees who have a birthday in the month.

Playing games.

Writing thank you cards to each other.

Doing meaningful activities together such as going to picnics, playing team building games, planting plants, cleaning the factory daily...

Agreeing on how to behave with each other.

Encouraging each member to find problems, discuss the root cause of the problem, and encourage people to propose a solution to the problem.

Agreeing that the next stage is the customer of the previous stage.

Teal Unicorn knows nothing about the manufacture of lingerie. We coach and train on the principles of Better Ways of Working and Managing, and suggest ideas to try based on those general principles. The solution lies within the staff and system of the client – we facilitate them finding it.

Results LOC achieved:

After doing a lot of gradual improvements over a period of nearly 5 months, most of the aforementioned problems have been resolved, the **productivity of LOC has increased by 68%** compared to the past. We are grateful to Mr. Rob and Cherry for guiding and consulting to help us continuously improve and always be asking: Can we be more lean? Can we do it better? Can we do it faster? Many questions are posed to find greater answers about breaking through, innovating, and further developing to meet our customers' demand better.

Most importantly, **we have built LOC into a family** where everyone feels they belong, where managers have learned how to be gardeners, where they look after and grow staff every day so they are constantly striving for the best quality and service for everyone who loves the products of LOC.

Teal Unicorn are so proud to be servants of Su and Loc. Su is a strong and dynamic woman who has made her own way against the resistance of Vietnamese culture, to be a successful liberated feminist woman beloved by her family and staff. Loc has supported and stood by her all the way, contributing his own intelligence as well. Cherry loves their beautiful comfortable products. They are now our friends.

A 2020 update

In January 2021, a newspaper article⁸⁴ appeared about LOC. Cherry reviewed it:

We are proud of you Su Nguyen and team LOC. After 3 times bringing the team to the Diggers game with Rob and Cherry to know how a self-

---

⁸⁴ https://thanhnien.vn/gioi-tre/co-gai-vuot-qua-dich-covid-19-1324465.html

organized lean factory should operate, and after how many days of perseverance on our coaching course, and learning how to sell agilely, and applying a salary-based skills policy ... you have led the team to overcome COVID-19 dramatically.

LOC not only did not experience a crisis, but also thrived in the face of disease and unfavorable markets.

Thank you, one of my golden girls.

Hopefully there will be many entrepreneurs who dare to change and apply agile thinking like her.

Ps / Cherry is a fan of LOC unwired underwear. Wearing it feels extremely comfortable and lovely. Highly recommended.

Here is our translation of the article:

Overcoming the Crisis of COVID-19

Su Nguyen, aged 28, debuted her brand of underwear with no frames 4 years ago. The idea now would hardly survive a year heavily affected by the COVID-19 epidemic, but Su Nguyen's products get ever more customers orders.

Set out many response scenarios

Nguyen Thi Nhuong, known as Su, set up a startup specializing in women's underwear in 2016. Because Su came from the medical sector, the frameless bra made by Su focused first on health, then usability, then fashion. Having only launched the product for a while, Su's brand attracted a lot of young girls, and also women who had given birth. Every few months, Su launched a new collection. From a 10-square-meter room with the first hand-crafted products made by her, up to now, when Su has a factory in Bien Hoa with several dozen specialized sewing machines and other machines, providing jobs for 42 employees.

With the general situation of the market, 2020 is a year full of fluctuations and challenges for individuals and especially businesses, especially small businesses. Su said: "As a former student in the specialized medical community, I came up with scenarios that could happen with the market and a business in the epidemic situation. As soon as it appeared in the New Year [*Tet: Lunar New Year in February*] of 2020, we had meetings continuously to rebuild our year plans. The first meeting with all the members of the company after Tet was to talk about the Covid-19 epidemic, and discuss. It is fortunate that the staff always accompany and unite with the company to prepare for a year of challenges ahead".

The company has no ranks, no positions

Financially, Su said, the company focused on optimizing resources, reducing costs from the smallest things like printing paper, disconnecting electricity when not needed …, collecting all cash to ensure that salaries could be maintained if the operation was forced to stop. At the same time, each month, they set aside a reserve fund to prevent risks occurring.

"In terms of people, instead of cutting staff, they will do more work. Each member will play many different roles… There are no ranks, no positions, and we only distinguish the skills that they have when they work. No one is too idle and no one is too busy. Allotted out for a smooth, unobstructed flow – fast fail – quick fix. Change to adapt, not wait for everything to pass", shared Su.

Change the way of doing, new approach

After a year of upheaval, Su realized that the world is constantly changing, each individual needs to be ready to change at any time to embrace the challenges ahead and always be creative and uplifting – leveled up to be better than yesterday.

"We should not stop, waiting for the difficulties to pass, but instead try to change the way of doing, the new approach. The challenge comes when individuals and businesses receive and learn a lot of lessons to survive and develop" Su said.

Sales peak month is twice as much as products' average

Thanks to the bravery, creativity and dynamism of the diminutive owner along with the unanimity of more than 40 members of the company, Su's no-rimmed underwear brand not only did not lose money, but on the contrary, it also maintained performance, with even more support from customers in the Covid-19 crisis.

Su received more online orders when overseas imports were banned. Currently, Su's brand has thousands of customers who became "fans" who regularly interact in Fanpage. And especially, members and customers recently joined hands to establish a Fan Club fund to share love to Da Nang during the epidemic and flooding in Central VietNam.

"2020 was a year when the members of the company have had days of highly strung tension, staying awake and pale, to research new products, new techniques, new ways from customer feedback. Difficulties and challenges for sure, but **in April at the peak of Covid-19 we sold 14,000 units while normally we sell only 7,000 units per month**. Our current factory is being expanded, with a new product line, with 42 young dynamic, enthusiastic and creative employees ", said Su.

LINHPOHS: Precious time
back through very human agile thinking

(Cẩm Lai in the long dress)

My name is Đỗ Cẩm Lai (Lucy Do), and I am CEO and owner of LINHPOHS[85], specializing in all kinds of shirts and home wear.

Time is my life and it is my most precious thing.

So to me, efficient use of time and agile management have helped me achieve success. Previously, I worked up to 12 hours / day, but in recent months, I only work 1-2 hours / day. Sometimes I have to remember to

---

[85] https://www.facebook.com/linhpohs/

call and ask the staff if they need any assistance. "Look, no sister !!!" but the efficiency is still increasing. I'm incredibly happy because the staff took my job away. Ooh ...

I'm not an expert, but I have the pleasure of sharing because maybe what I write can touch someone, helping them get out of a deadlock like I used to be in.

A while ago, my best friend Hang shared that every time Vinh Duc Real Estate has a successful transaction, the whole company will gather to celebrate in the real sense. I thought to myself: "My God, what company congratulates each other on their success so much. People from human resources, accounting, and all sales members, they are all happy together when a deal is closed. What do we do? But does that way of working really exist in the world? "

Today is our turn to be happy together. Often, from one employee to the other, employees call out "Yay, first order 20 items" / "ha ha ... 50 items" / "OMG, 100 items ..." Just cheering voices all over. A young staffer was busy packing the orders while exclaiming gleefully, "My hands are so happy packing" ... You may be surprised that my staff do not even get commission from the sales because I pay a big salary instead. I motivate them by giving things which have *more value th*an money such as:

1. Giving them parenting training courses online.

2. Giving English courses to part-time staff who are going to be preschool teachers.

3. Paying club memberships for women to be more beautiful and happier.

4. Supporting the tuition fees for the children of staff who are enrolling in better schools.

5. Sending staff to sales training courses.

6. Subsidising staff to buy iPhones so they can enjoy and work more effectively.

7. Funding travelling.

8. Accepting children and grandchildren of the staff to join our team.

9. Giving gifts to employees' children occasionally.

10. Facilitate selling their yogurt.

11. Scheduling first aid training courses on common accidents in the family with Survival Skills Vietnam.

In general, I am quite altruistic. The reason I have a lot of time is thanks to employee management according to agile thinking and methods. I just put in requirements only, the employees manage themselves in their own way, and I welcome failure and always work with them on what we learn from that, what we can do and build a procedure for better execution in future. And my staff work even better than me, so don't think about using your own experience to teach the staff everything. That's wrong!

My staff go to work with HAPPINESS every day, so I am successful. Money is not a successful destination for me.

The secret lies in the "agile Management" course from Cherry Vu and Rob England.

I would like to share a few points:

1. Agile management thinking: why it resonates for me.

Previously, I always looked for solutions to "handle" unmotivated employees, employees who did not have the spirit of learning, employees who made excuses when doing wrong ... all my objectives were aimed at correcting employees. Hearing and witnessing how a better way looks after my best friend Hang applied Agile Management inspired me to go find out. The happiness of each employee at Vinh Duc Real Estate spreads to its founder and has spread to me. I wanted to bring that happiness back to my employees.

2. What changes have I made to my organization after seeing Cherry's Agile Thinking? And does it work?

– The first and biggest change is to change the manager's way of thinking. Now that I look back, I can imagine what Cherry was thinking when listening to my purpose for the course when we first introduced ourselves. "My organisation has a problem that is all due to the staff". Later I realised that I wasn't thinking scientifically, I did not understand the cause of the problem, that the error lies in the system, the procedures.

– The way I interact with employees has changed from orders to dialogue. Our response to mistakes starts from: Why is it going wrong? Where is the missing process? or we look at the communication: the employees have not understood? In the past, not only did I identify the wrong person, but I told them off and punished them. Now, it helps employees feel safe to talk about all the problems to you, because they know you will help them instead of punishing them. There is always a so-called cost of mistakes, which also comes from your system, exposing you to where to fix it.

– Managers are not above looking: I go to where they work and look at their work – go to gemba. There are problems that cannot be solved over the phone, no matter how many times I call, but when meeting them, listening to them speak, asking questions to understand the nature, I have a deeper insight and knowledge of the issue. Problems and solutions appear right after that.

– Pursuing quality to have agility: To avoid ending up having to cut costs and make layoffs, I had resisted hiring more people so we wouldn't have that risk when the market is slow. I had a shortage of people, so my organization was always in a state of overload. After understanding that I was thinking wrongly, I listed out the overloaded jobs and priorities to do in the coming time in order to set direction in recruiting people. With the ability to do each other's work, they create more value, productivity increases dramatically, and the risks and costs go down as a result.

– When studying the Teal Unicorn training and coaching, I realised that the staff are the ones directly creating value. Because of urgency or lack of someone available, I used to agree to let the garment staff deliver when needed, resulting in their work being interrupted. After the class, I informed the workshop to stop the waste, and found a delivery man to take over.

– To flexibly handle jobs and not lose any, I created small groups such as: closing orders, dividing rows, composing orders, orders urgently needed by customers, adjustments at work ... Each time if problems arise, employees self-classify and send requests with pictures to the appropriate group so that those involved will take the job and handle it. Whoever handles what will drop a heart/like on the message/image assigned to that task. After this, we can check who has done it to verify and sit back and find solutions.

– Flow of work: When Cherry taught us about value stream mapping, I applied it immediately, and now I always use this method since I understand its value. When I see the flow from planning -> cutting -> printing -> sewing, I can see the wastes through each step, grasp the waiting time, understand where the work is stuck ... That provides a general picture for me so I can adjust it and prioritise work better at the right time. However, it is necessary for many parts to work together, so some parties are not consistent when implementing. It is necessary to introduce better policies and call for commitments to implement.

– With Teal Unicorn's agile Sales training, I like the idea that customers who complain can mean they care. They can be potential customers, they want to buy so they complain about this and that. Before then, I considered them to be annoying and mercilessly overlooked them, but when studying Agile Sales I changed my mind. I patiently answered customer inquiries, and went back to where I lacked a response as soon as possible. Since then, I do not mind how difficult it is to handle such cases and thereby grow a lot of loyal customers – which is also a point that customers appreciate about us. The staff too are welcoming complaints with great politeness and patience.

– Authority And Trust: In the past, I used to work with detailed requirements and use my own experience to force employees to follow my way of doing it. Later, I realised that if I do that, the employee road is very narrow, their creativity is limited. I had done it a lot, so I knew a lot was completely wrong. Employees are people who are deeply involved in their work, they are my work improvers. I assign them to organize their own storage, as long as they explain why they did – I nod if I feel it is reasonable. Photographers are the same, they always have novel ideas, shooting angles and set ups that I have difficulty keeping up with. Employees plan the sales setups and explain the reasons for them to make such a decision, if something is not right, then work with them ... You will learn a lot from employees if you accept it is ok for them to get it wrong, to mature employees together with you, and then trust and learn from them.

– Multi-functions for each employee: in the past I thought specialisation was professional, but later realised multi-ability is even more advanced. I allocate a short time during each day for employees to guide each other's work, get acquainted, and share how. The effect is that when an employee realises that someone is sick, they can jump over to support without stopping the flow, and when you need to focus on another stage you can switch jobs by yourself. A supporting culture was born from there, but people still needed a bond with a common goal and LamLuy, another practitioner in the Agile Management community, helped me realise that. [*It makes us very happy that the tribe of students are helping each other. LamLuy's story is in this collection too.*]

3. How effective is agile management in my organisation? I would like to demonstrate by numbers.

I was "enlightened" in May 2020 by agile thinking. Looking at the statistics you will see that **sales from May increased steadily towards the end of the year.**

After applying agile thinking, the highest revenue month (October 2020) is 4.5 times higher than the low revenue month (March 2020).

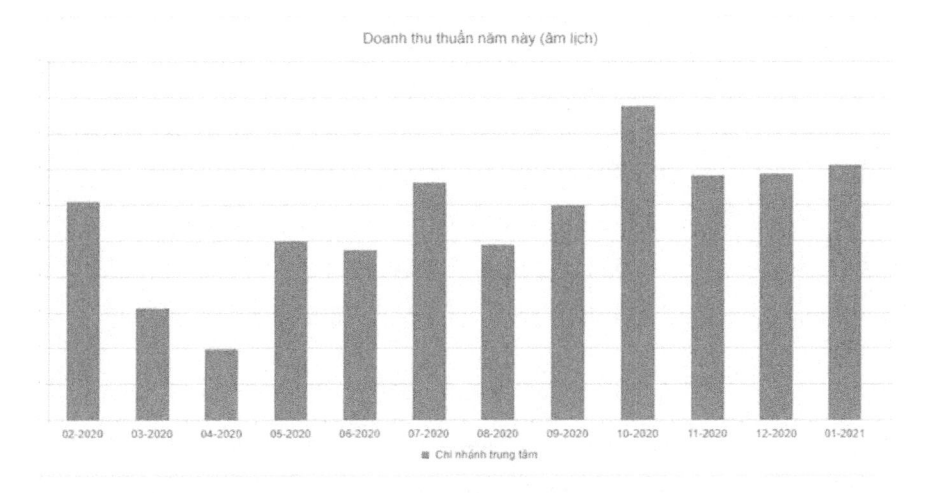

Doanh thu thuần năm này (âm lịch)

■ Chi nhánh trung tâm

Part Two: LINHPOHS

In 9 years of operation, the market was the most turbulent in 2020. It was a difficult time, everyone cut down on spending, especially the needs like clothing. A lot of stores have evaporated. **But we got the highest revenue ever, at a time of COVID** – I look back and think wow!

In the last 4 consecutive months (from October 2020 to January 2021), revenue has been higher than previous months.

4. How has my organization's emotions, behavior, and culture changed since I caught this new wave of thinking?

Life is a series of choices. If I had continued following the mindset of being the boss, only interested in numbers, exhausting people to achieve goals, and indifferent to the spiritual life of subordinates, or in other words motivating them with my own pressure, I believe I wouldn't have been able to last until today. My mindset is not making money at all costs, so my biggest success is the HAPPINESS of my employees. Everyone comes here as a family where they feel belonging, trusted, respected, loved, and sharing. Always filled with laughter at work, at least they are happy for 8 hours / day. When I fell into such a happy paradise, I was dosed with dopamine every day – a formidable contagious hormone of happiness. In my organisation there was an employee who had a negative view of everything, she always wanted more money because she was poor. She has transformed into a sharing, caring person now. I was deeply moved when she used her own salary to buy diapers, toys, and food for other employees. Dr Cherry is right, when staff are happy, productivity naturally increases: productivity in work and productivity in "giving".

[Cam Lai is a lovely person. She was managing in the way she thought managers were supposed to manage, but it wasn't her real self. The strain of the cognitive dissonance was breaking her. Cherry set her free.]

Happy staff, happy owner. I have more time to make customers happier with my new policies and ideas. "Free", I think of ways to bring so much value to my teammates and thank them very much for giving me a lot of time to live with my passion – Education. *[Cam Lai now has time to start a whole new education business, but that's another story.]*

It is wonderful – very human agile thinking, Cherry and Rob !!!

ERICK: Real and effective

ways of managing and working

Hoang Tuấn Anh owns and runs a business supplying equipment for beauty spas. He came to Cherry in October 2020 to join the coaching course for agile managers every Sunday. Then Tuấn Anh brought his team on a training course to become agile managers. Agile manager, agile business. When I coached Tuấn Anh, I "assigned exercises" to him: With the smaller scale of ERICK[86], I challenged him to transform from the present state to an agile business within three months.

---

[86] https://erick.vn/

Part Two: ERICK

And Tuấn Anh not only did not disappoint me but he is my pride and joy. I am really happy because of what Tuấn Anh and ERICK team have done, the joy of a gardener.

This is what Tuấn Anh and ERICK did.

What is the reason for you to seek an agile management mindset?

After trying to apply a lot of other management methods that are costly, time consuming and resource-hungry, but the results are very limited, I have come to an agile management approach and I have found it real and effective.

What changes have you tried since you learned about agile management from Cherry?

Some activities I am doing:

– All members of the organization have learned about agile management and implemented together

– I have changed my leadership mindset from "leadership thinking" to "leadership thinking accompanying teammates", changed from "administrative thinking" to "agile management thinking", from "centralized thinking" to "empower and encouragement". Our working method is changed from "professional mode" to "main professional mode with versatile and agile work".

– We organize Lean Coffee sessions that we call TalkShow so that everyone can share their problems and plan to solve together.

– We hold stand-up meetings every day.

– We build by trial and error, try quickly and welcome new ideas.

– We reduce work time so team members have time to improve performance.

– We listen and find consensus from members.

– As a manager, I provide transparent information at every step, so that the members can understand the situation and promote collective intelligence.

What worked and what didn't?

Things that really work:

– When I switched from one form of leadership to another, I felt better collective cohesion.

– When moving from "administrative type management, specialization" to "agile management and versatile", I see the members improve their skills better and collectively adapt to new problems.

– When moving from centralized management to empowerment, I see that the members are more proactive and creative, reducing bureaucracy and internal conflicts.

– Lean Coffee and the stand-up meeting help us keep informed. People are ready to better support each other, and the organization becomes more agile.

– Tools like Kanban help us get to the job a lot better than before.

– Listening and finding consensus helps us to understand each other and have a strong internal connection.

Things that haven't really worked yet:

– "Try new things" are always our tough challenges, sometimes our members are still blocked by old habits and old ways.

– "Measuring results by indicators" is something we have not done thoroughly, there are many things we have not given specific indicators to evaluate.

What improvements have you made successfully? What was the result?

Business results in the last 2 months of 2020 (since I started applying agile management) **reached 150% and 200% over the same period in 2019.**

How has your organization's behavior and culture changed since you adopted this new mindset?

+ Positive feelings and solidarity among members.

+ Members focus on work and efficiency improves markedly.

+ Members have a clear sense of the "corporate culture", the difference and the positive of the current business compared to other businesses.

+ The members believe in the future development of the enterprise based on a truly effective and humane management method.

Can you compare Teal Unicorn's ideas with other improvements you've tried in the past?

+ The ideas of Teal Unicorn is the BEST humanitarian management method I have ever approached. Teal Unicorn helps to perfect individual skills, each member of the organization can live truly "whole". They are improving themselves continuously.

+ The ideas of Teal Unicorn help us to unleash collective intelligence, many improvement ideas. Members become united, ready to support each other.

+ Teal Unicorn helps us truly become an agile group, increasing the team's adaptability to the constant fluctuations of the market.

LamLuy: Working

more efficiently, and happily

These two talented young and beautiful girls are Lũy Phạm and Nhi Lâm, the owners of Lamluy[87], unique designer lingerie. I was going to post a picture of myself [Cherry] wearing Lamluy's clothes but I was too scared.

---

[87] https://lamluy.vn/

Part Two: LamLuy

What is the reason you turn to an agile management mindset?

The desire to build a team that works less, is more efficient, and happier.

What changes have you tried since you learned about agile management from Cherry?

Changing bonus policy, employees feel happier.

In the past, we used to share rewards individually, and only reward commissions for sales staff, the rest of the department was not related to sales. This leads to the sales people competing with each other, with less support for each other. When one of them has achieved personal sales targets, there is no motivation to try more. The positions and divisions have no link or are not wholeheartedly supporting each other.

After studying Dr Cherry, realising the ineffectiveness of the current policy, and the sense that each member must connect with each other and connect with the common results, Lamluy changed the "individual reward" policy to "bonus team" (all positions from sales, customer care, warehouse, packaging ...). And they are the ones who discuss and decide how to divide the reward.

The results they shared are that "I feel fairer and happier for every order I sell, I am aware that it is the team effort, and everyone has a part in it. We need to support each other to achieve a common goal."

Small and continuous testing, small and continuous improvement

Previously, due to our small scale, we also produced quite a bit in each production phase. But after learning about agile management, as we get bigger, we are always conscious of applying this principle thoroughly.

Every time we launch a new product line, we produce a small amount for customers to use, get feedback, and then we rely on it to improve for the next production. Continuing with the "Plan – Do – Check – Act" circle, it is the customer who clearly tells us what they want, and we have the opportunity to find a solution to perfect the product, or do research, developing new products to meet the needs of customers more.

For example, in the launch of a brand new product recently – Lamluy T-shirts - we tried it on with existing customers who had already used our products, and received very positive feedback, confirming the shirt design. At the same time, we also received suggestions to perfect the shirt to meet the needs of customers, so that we could confidently launch officially and introduce it to new customers. As a result, the new design was very well received, with 65% of production being sold within 20 days.

Rebuild sales processes, focus on customers. And give HR the tools and knowledge they need.

Previously, Lamluy had a sales process, but it was still quite sketchy, and did not meet all the needs of customers. The sales manager lacked the tools and knowledge to do their position and role well.

After learning and understanding agile sales [*a Teal Unicorn course*], as well as customer-centricity, Lamluy team gathered and together defined more clearly what customers need in each sales consultation, and what the sales staff need. Hang [*from Vinh Duc Real Estate*] also recommended the knowledge and tools that she needs to do a good job.

Based on that, we rebuilt the Sales Process, product documentation, collection documents, then conducted training and deployment.

Sales people feel it is easier to advise and share with customers more fully and attractively about each product line, each collection.

Customer feedback is more positive, often complimenting the enthusiasm and thoughtfulness of the Sales staff, who talk about Lamluy more with the customers.

Autonomous team, multi-function, high-link

Previously, when the Lamluy team was very small, there was still a lot of confusion, sometimes versatile, sometimes rigid, everyone did anything, depending on management. Compared to a year ago, currently the number of personnel has doubled and become more agile, autonomous, and multi-functional:

There is no manager position. Tasks are divided according to skills, and roles. The positions are interchangeable: the Sales Officer can also work as the Warehouse Officer or Packing Officer; customer care staff can also sell goods, all positions take care of customers ... When needed, this position can completely do the work of another position.

Staff analyze and set goals for themselves, plan together, and support each other to achieve common goals. The positions are all interactive, it is easy and quick to discuss with each other to solve work.

There is a standup meeting for 10-15 minutes a day for the flow of information to be smooth. Each of them proactively raise problems for the whole team to discuss and work out solutions.

They get feedback on the output of their work and decide for themselves how to do their job, without micro management, and are encouraged to try and fail to the extent allowed. Because they are empowered, more of them are creative, happier and harder working.

Turning the [*hierarchical*] pyramid upside down, we always support employees to create value. Instead of micro management, we focus on finding and removing barriers, improving systems and policies so that our staff can be better and happier with their work.

Get out of the way for employees who create value, do their jobs well, don't impose on them.

Nurturing a safe mentality, staff are free to voice their thoughts, suggestions and ideas.

What worked and what didn't?

All the things we've tried have worked, or if not, after a few adjustments it will work.

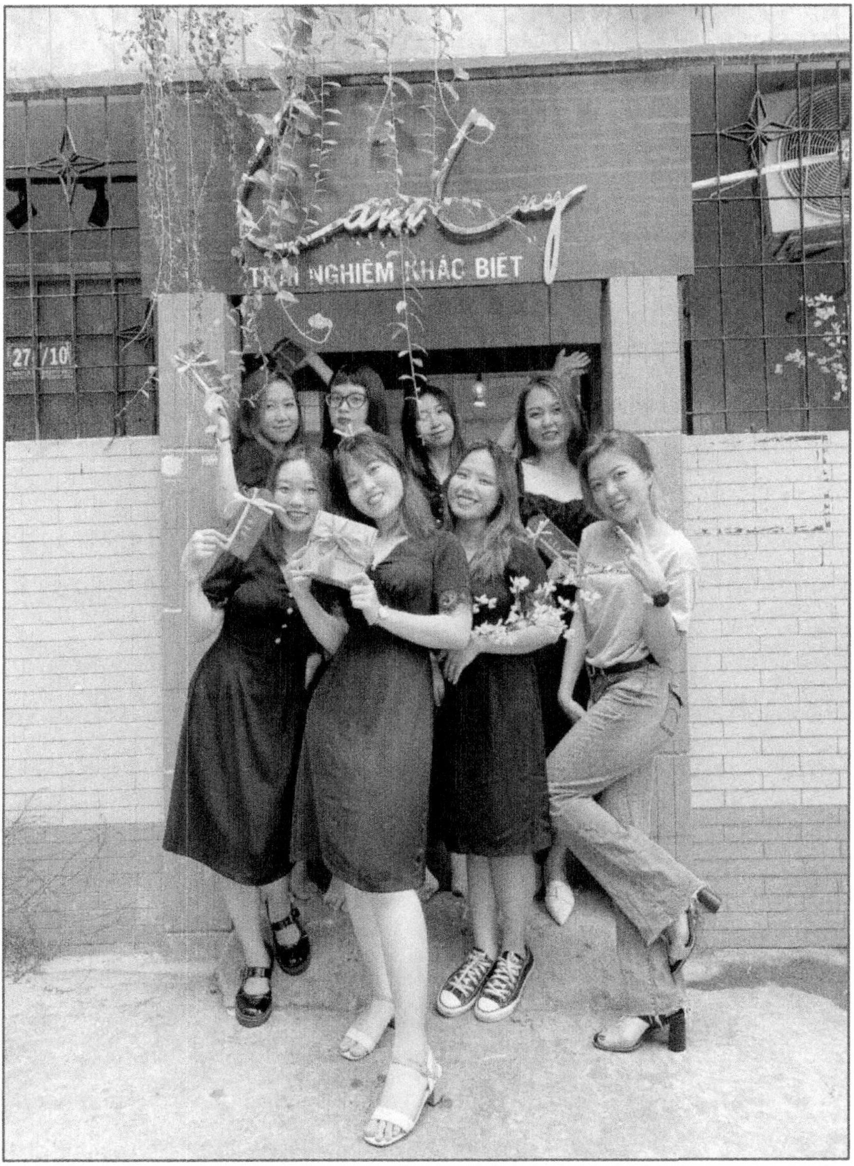
NGHIỆM KHÁC BIỆT
27/10

What improvements have you made successfully? What was the result?

Specifically, the flow of work at the factory, after many adjustments, is clearer, faster and smoother. **As a result, production output in 2020 increased by 90% compared to 2019 with the same number of employees. Factory income in 2020 increased 84% compared to 2019.**

The operations team work more efficiently and happily, set monthly revenue targets, self-plan the implementation, proactively support and help support each other, and they can replace each other's positions to achieve the same goals. As a result, **revenue in 2020 grew 115% compared to 2019. Profits in 2020 grew by 320% compared to 2019.**

How have emotions, behavior and culture of your organization changed since you adopted this new mindset?

All members are proactive in their work and actively support other members to accomplish common goals.

The more comfortable and confident staff can propose to make the work more creative, efficient, and more customer focused. They shared that they were satisfied with the results and wanted to contribute more to Lamluy. You are very creative in your work when you have the autonomy to decide how to do it. The staff increasingly connects and loves and helps each other.

Can you compare Teal Unicorn's idea with other improvements you have tried in the past?

Compared to the old way of working, we are more and more efficient, achieving more in terms of both people and sales and profits. The team achieved its goal of working more efficiently, and happily.

Đồ lót thiết kế độc đáo

Teal Unicorn in Vietnam

Finally for Part Two, here is an article that appeared in the Business Agility Institute's regular journal, Emergence, giving a personal perspective from Rob on Cherry's work in Vietnam. Sorry, it does repeat a few bits from the rest of this book.

Vietnam is a nation in a state of rapid change and growth. GDP has doubled since 2010 to over US$270 billion. Prosperity and wellbeing are up on almost all measures. The culture is still deeply conservative and authoritarian, with social change lagging behind economic progress. Shut off behind a language barrier deeper than most Asian countries, the ideas that we share in the BAI community are unfamiliar in Vietnam. There is a small Agile community in software development, but it struggles against the conventional thinking, and Agile certainly hasn't escaped to the wider enterprise. The illustrated edition of Laloux's book, *Reinventing Organizations*, was translated into Vietnamese, but very few other works have been.

In 2018, Dr Cherry Vu (T.S. Vũ Anh Đào) started going from New Zealand to Vietnam, to teach, coach, and consult on the ideas of business agility. I have the opportunity to observe Dr Vu at work every day as Dr Vu is not only my business partner, but also my wife. We call ourselves Teal Unicorn: it is just us, with associates helping us out from time to time. I won't even pretend to be objective about her, but the facts I share here are real. The results our clients get are so good that we have difficulty overcoming the justifiable scepticism of anything written by a consultancy about themselves. We are not selling – we have no need of more work. We want you to know that business agility really works. The test is in the reaction of our clients, who continue to expand their engagement with Cherry, forming a tribe around her, helping each other, some of them becoming our personal friends. A US$2.5 billion corporation is currently growing their engagement with us, drawing in even the Board and the CEO. The immediate financial results convince them. At the same time, we continue to help a yoga studio, a coffee shop, and a school. Dr Vu works with clients ranging from the largest banks, manufacturers, and logistics companies to small retailers and SMEs, from businesses with five employees to those with 25,000. Dr Vu combines common sense advice with extensive business experience and knowledge of modern ways of thinking, working, and managing that boost business performance, staff morale, and organisational values. The world commonly calls these ways of thinking "agile".

Those Cherry has worked with report the following results attributed to these better ways:

- A clothing manufacturer overcame constraints to increase clothing production by 90% in 2020 as compared to 2019 with the same number of employees, and throughout the COVID-19 pandemic. Revenue grew by 115% year over year. Profits up 320%.
- Cost and time of approvals processes reduced by 80% or more in a large manufacturer.
- A bank branch increased their sales performance by 158% over a period of ten weeks in 2021. They achieved their annual quota in those ten weeks and were named the top performing bank branch for their bank, nationwide.
- Equipment sales increased by five times over five months in 2020. Making a profit, at last.
- Fashion sales: highest revenue month (October 2020) is 4.49 times higher than the previous highest revenue month (March 2020), while in the middle of COVID.
- A lingerie manufacturer revamped their workflow and increased productivity by 150%, while successfully clearing their

backlogged inventory in two weeks. In April 2020, they sold 14,000 units as compared to 7,000 units per month normally.
- In 2021, 4 staff are selling as much real estate as 45 used to in 2019.

More important to us are the personal impacts we have in people's lives. We helped Hang simplify her real estate agency, improve it, and make more money, all while delivering her first baby. We helped Su turn a struggling lingerie business into a booming one, proving her doubters wrong. We helped Cam Lai have happier staff, be the person she wanted to be, and thrive amidst the pandemic. We helped Huyen blow some of the cobwebs out of a giant manufacturer she was born into, so she could retire happier. We helped Tuan Anh get his sales and distribution staff engaged and motivated, to save his company. You can read these case studies at tealunicorn.com/clients

At the core of these success stories are key changes in mindset and values that many coaches will recognise as universally applicable. Some of the changes that Dr Vu coaches her clients toward include:

- Team goals, not individual. Work as a team, assess as a team, and reward as a team.
- Collaborative rituals within and across teams, e.g. OpenSpace.
- Change how managers manage. Invert the hierarchy through servant management and invitational management.
- "Skills not roles" allows for fluidity of work. Let people self-assess as Shu-Ha-Ri, with peer review.
- Self-organising and self-assembling teams leads to fluidity of structure.
- Cross-functional teams. Try Team Tetris: start with who you have and stop trying to mold people into standard shapes.
- Empower workers and get out of the way. Let the people doing the work design the work.

- Open the books and be transparent about finances. Let staff work out how to apportion pay: first the bonuses, and the salary later.
- Pay people to leave. Work harder at recruiting the right people.
- Be better people; embrace integrity, ethics, respect, transparency, humanocracy, values over value, and stakeholder capitalism.

We jokingly call these shifts in mindset, values and outlook the Teal Unicorn "secret formula", because it is so secret that - like all good secrets - it is on the internet, at tealunicorn.com/our-secret-formula. If you promise not to tell anyone, I will share it here:

- You can't make people do good work. You can only invite, motivate, and inspire, then get out of the way.
- Respect, empower, and trust your staff.
- Be better people.
- Make work better.
- Embrace failure.
- Fix the system, not the individual.
- Ask questions, don't tell.
- Don't try too much. Go step by step. Experiment locally.
- There is no standard template.
- You don't need to believe or trust me. Try it.

Adoption of these shifts in mindset requires shifts in practice. Again, these changes apply universally, and not only to the Vietnamese business landscape. How we get these ideas adopted is equally secret, at tealunicorn.com/how-we-make-a-difference. Again, I'll confidentially share a summary here:

- Visualise work.
- Communicate.
- Create some headroom.
- Explore the delivery value stream(s) together.

- Visualise flow of work.
- Wait for the pennies to drop: management is part of the problem.
- Broker a common set of values and principles to work by.
- Introduce the ideas of new ways of working, and new ways of managing.
- Focus on creating more headroom.
- Start experimenting.
- Create an improvement "machine".
- Create bubbles of new ways.
- Find triads of mutually supporting peers.
- Create - or wait for - an executive mandate.
- Start an invitational (pull, don't push) movement for wider adoption.

For many of you reading this, there is nothing new there. But for just as many of you, I'll wager you struggle to get it to happen.

Understanding why it works

I have examined and rejected several hypotheses as to why Dr Vu is so effective.

The first hypothesis is that Vietnam is somehow culturally different. Of course, all cultures have their differences. Vietnam has a few obvious ones: Communism, Confucianism, and corruption for a start. But once you live amongst multiple cultures, you realise that people are people. There are all kinds everywhere. The cultural differences between Vietnam and New Zealand feel no more extreme than the differences between New Zealand and the USA.

Teal Unicorn's tribe of Vietnamese clients are not typical either. They are very much culturally aligned with Teal Unicorn. They are a self-selecting group: Teal Unicorn doesn't do any marketing or sales - our clients approach us. Our schedules are full: we are not looking for work.

In a country of 100 million people, there are plenty of organisations for whom these ideas resonate, even if they form a small minority of the whole country. The same would be true anywhere else in the world: the key is not the national culture but the culture of those organisations that choose to work with you, and that you choose to work with. Dr Vu has declined to work with several clients because they were not ready for these ideas.

A corollary of this is the hypothesis that it *only* works with people who are already open to these ideas. But that is not the case either. Individuals seek out assistance for many reasons: they come to our training, or start interacting with us within their organisation, or hear about us. Their motives can be curiosity or greed as often as passion for the new ideas. Even people for whom the ideas of agility don't resonate can see the financial benefits of changing how they manage and how they work. Behaviour becomes belief, and Dr Vu hopes that, over time, her clients will change their nature too.

Could Dr Vu's success rely on her only working with the biggest boss in the organisation, preferably the owner? While it is true that Dr Vu often has that level of access which helps immensely, Teal Unicorn also works with large organisations where access is more restricted. That said, access opens up pretty quickly once you start demonstrating results. So this hypothesis is at least partly true.

Another hypothesis is that it only works with women. It is true that three-quarters of Teal Unicorn's key sponsors and relationship owners within our client list are women. There may indeed be a cultural factor at work here, in that Vietnam is often a sexist country; many men in Vietnam don't like being given advice by a woman. There is also the fact that modern ways of thinking and managing are more stereotypically feminine, as Dana Ardi wrote in her book *The Fall of the Alphas*. Dr Vu rejects this idea: she finds that many men are open to these ideas, and some of her best clients are men. We should not use gender stereotypes to classify or target people. Men who are prepared to think in these new ways are the men of our future, who we should embrace without getting hung up on gender. I'm as proud to exhibit stereotypically feminine traits as I am to be a woke snowflake. I try hard to be a gender role model in Vietnam. I have happy memories of the funny misunderstandings that resulted until people realised that Cherry is in charge in Vietnam. I just carry the bags and make the games work.

Yet another hypothesis is that Vietnam does business so badly that Dr Vu's clients were starting from a very low level; in other words, she had the luxury of picking low-hanging fruit. It is easy to think this way when you see some of the things that Teal Unicorn has helped correct. Yet in comparison with our experience of the levels of practice in other countries, Vietnam doesn't come out looking so bad compared to so-called developed nations. Awful management and work practices are clearly global. In fact, visitors to Vietnam often notice how modern, orderly, and smoothly functioning it all is, which, considering the amount of money siphoned off by corruption, and that the country was shattered and starving in the 1980s, means they must be doing everything else right.

A trickier hypothesis is that Cherry is special. This is harder to reject. She has a diverse business background. She has moved in powerful circles and is highly respected, earning her the trust of some of the most influential people in Vietnam. She is a strong personality with high integrity. It certainly makes a great deal of difference in persuading people. Our corporate clients have had the usual suspects in: Deloittes, McKinsey et al. They all report that it achieved little and cost a lot. I'm sure those firms employ very high calibre people but it doesn't seem to work. So it is just possible that Cherry is the secret ingredient. Much as I love her, I hope not. I have had success with these ideas in New Zealand, albeit at lower levels in organisations, primarily within IT. I've seen other consultants make great organisational change around the world, and one reads about them in books and online, not least through the Business Agility Institute. Let's assume that it's not unique to Dr Vu, even if I can't entirely rule it out.

At a macro level, more generally, there are two connected hypotheses as to why these better ways work so well.

First: you can't change how you work until you change how you manage. To unlock organisations' path to better ways of working, the key is better ways of managing. By focusing on changing the ways of management in an organisation, we succeed in rapidly unlocking the potential of the workers to achieve far more than they would otherwise be able.

Think of all the "transformations", the attempts to introduce new ways of working, that you have seen fail. I believe almost *all* those I have seen fail did so because management didn't change how they manage the work.

The second hypothesis: globally, management thinking has been ruined by a culture which has emerged progressively (or rather, regressively) throughout the course of the 20th Century. It has its roots in Taylorism and scientific management. It became captured by bureaucracy as the human world grew massively in scale, and corporations became the dominant structure. Finally, management has become corrupted by Friedmanism and the global rise of unfettered capitalism, of right-wing greed, in the last few decades of the 20th Century.

The result of this is dehumanised command-and-control management, which diminishes people and disempowers them. In its worst extremes, we say that organisations burn people for fuel. The social contract between employer and employee is widely broken - neither trusts the other. While conventional management used to deliver results, the whole structure in crumbling in the face of:

- rising numbers of knowledge workers (for whom it simply doesn't work, you can't make them do anything).
- the increasing volatility of the world after seventy years of relative stability.
- the insane acceleration in the rate of change of biological, materials, and digital technologies.
- a resurgence of progressive social values and expectations.

Managers are as much trapped in the system of work as the workers are. Psychopathy becomes selected for in conventional management systems, so that it is over-represented relative to the general population, but psychopaths are still a minority of managers. Most managers are good people who exhibit delight and relief when they are allowed to behave in better ways when managing people. One of the biggest changes in how they manage is to be nice. Change the management culture from power to invitation; from dominion to inclusion; from force to respect; from suspicion to trust; from anger to affection; from commanders to gardeners.

Dr Vu gets little resistance to cultural change from managers once they understand what it really means. She does of course get the initial resistance of middle management simply because their primary function is to suppress risk and resist change. Occasionally the immune system of the organisation defeats change entirely: we have two clients where our engagement ended despite the results. But breaking through is possible when managers see that executives are walking the walk; when they see the results in both the performance and morale of the people they are responsible for; and, most of all, when they see how we are reducing organisational risk, not increasing it.

Dr Vu doesn't approach organizations with a message of eliminating managers. She has a great deal of respect and appreciation for the essential role of management in an organisation. Dr Vu's message is that what got you here won't get you there: that you need to manage differently, not throw the managers overboard. Teal Unicorn presents less of a threat to managers. (That's not to say that some organisations don't end up with fewer managers, but that is not the goal. You make better use of managers, managing the right things in the right ways.)

Both of these hypotheses - managers are the lock and management behaviour is the key - are supported by some of the leading thinkers in work and management. Dr Vu draws inspiration and enlightenment from books such as:

- Edwards Deming's *Out of the Crisis*.
- Peter Drucker's *Management* (and others).
- Frederic Laloux's *Reinventing Organizations*.
- Stan McChrystal's *Team of Teams*.
- Steve Denning's *The Age of Agile*.
- Aaron Dignan's *Brave New Work*.
- Gary Hamel's and Michele Zanini's *Humanocracy*.
- Jonathan Smart's *Sooner Safer Happier*.

We would never have come up with it on our own. We don't so much stand on the shoulders of giants as cling to their coattails. We have enduring gratitude for all the great thinkers have given us the gift of better ways. Beneath the better ways of managing and working are better ways of thinking, as humanity continues its multi-millennium cultural advance. Discussing the reunification of truth, beauty, and goodness, would be another article entirely. Suffice to say that these ideas go deeper than management practice.

One final possibility is that Teal Unicorn's unconventional style of consulting is the critical factor that accelerates change in behaviour. Again, I reiterate this isn't a sales pitch: we have plenty of work. It is important to understand how business agility thinking should reflect on consulting as much as on the clients. I hope it is clear from the tone of this article that we go out of our way not to be part of conventional corporate consulting culture. If we are to evangelise better ways of thinking and working, we need to live them and model them ourselves.

- Our work is invitational: if people don't want the new ways, we don't push the issue. We go somewhere where they do. The people who come are the right people. Change must be pulled not pushed.
- We don't know the answers. Nobody does, no matter how much you pay them. We bring principles, patterns, and methods that clients can use to find their own answer, unique to their organisation, and found within it.
- We talk as much about integrity and morality as we do about flow and experiment. Better work requires better people.
- Work is political and sociological. You cannot separate them anymore. To be whole at work, we must feel our values align with the values of our employer, and we should feel safe to say when they don't.
- We teach empowerment of others, and personal agency. We undermine the assumed authority of seniority and title. We call out bosses and encourage assertion in staff (diplomatically of course). The new prosperity means people are ready for better lives, especially the young. We are both in a second marriage, which is shocking in Vietnam.
- We are a couple: we support each other emotionally and physically in the classroom. We bring our whole selves. Emotions are real and present, not repressed. We are genuine in caring.

People cry. We take our pastoral duties seriously with our tribe of customers.

Obviously, we think there is some truth in this hypothesis. We believe in the better ways of working which we are imparting to clients, so naturally we believe embracing these principles at work makes us more effective: humanity, whole self, inclusion, invitation, empowerment, equity, passion. We leave it to the reader to judge.

This picture was taken by our photographer during a course in Vietnam, while a student was presenting something emotionally powerful.

Part Three: ELABORATION

The many endnotes and explanations of the concepts introduced in Part One.

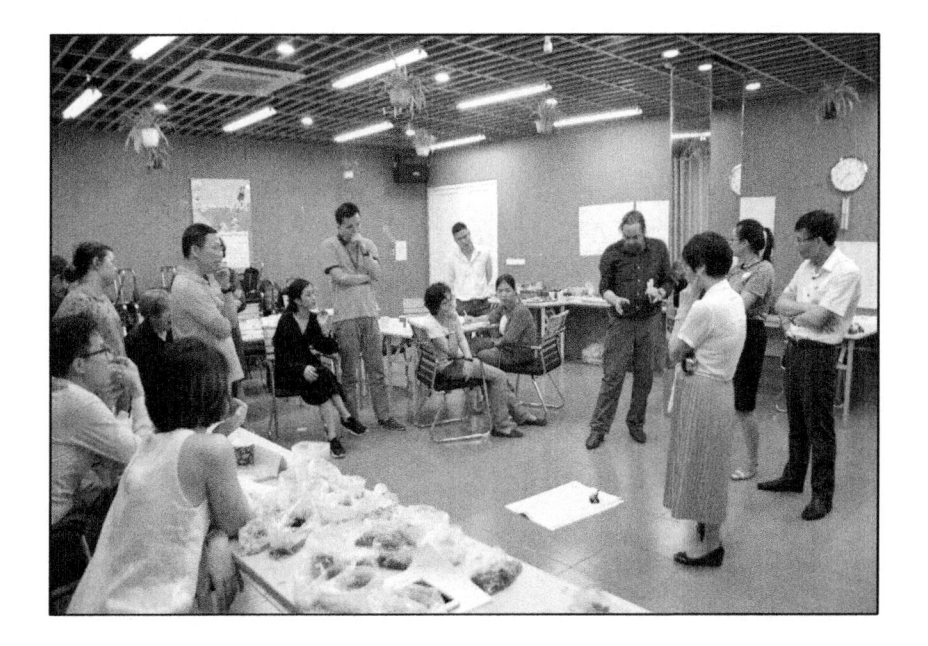

Part Three

You've read Part One, the core book, then Part Two, the storytelling. Now what follows is Part Three, the endnotes, a collection of ideas expanding on topics in Part One and referenced from there. As a result, they don't always flow on from each other in a cohesive narrative, but I have tried to group them to make some sense as you read through them. The main headings are:

> Open Work: how work opens up in better ways.
> Open Management: how managers behave differently.
> Open Thinking: the philosophical ideas underpinning it all.

You can find out much more about these topics in the companion book, *The agile (small a)*, and on the website, tealunicorn.com.

Open Work

We must open up how we work.

- Let the light in: be transparent, visualise work, be real, be honest, be vulnerable.
- Let people in: be inclusive, encourage diversity.
- Give people room: get out of the way, empower, liberate.
- Let people connect: remove silos, encourage collaboration, create networks.

Human Systems Adaptability

I went looking for a term for the better, open ways of working. I came up with nothing, so I created a word cloud of ideas and organised it. I identified three key themes to the better ways of working:

Human: people, values, humanity, wholeness, culture, sharing, empathy, diversity, inclusiveness, egality, trust, integrity, authenticity, open, transparency, curiosity, learning, mastery, pride, empowerment, freedom, authorisation, servant manager, safety, wellbeing, flourishing, health. [states]

Systems: customer, value, flow, feedback, quality, lean, streams, iteration, networks, complexity, chaos, tensions, emergence, antifragile, shift left, teams, organisation, collaboration, ritual, sharing, resilience, human error, holistic, data, science. [artefacts]

Adaptability: ambiguous, uncertain, contradictory, iterate, increment, experiment, explore, observe, adjust, agile, fluid, organic, improve, curious, embrace failure, fail fast, small, granular, simplify, flexible, pragmatic, resilient. [actions/adjectives]

Humanity

The movement to make the workplace more human is real. Most employers now value emotional intelligence over intellect[88]. Soft skills (what a terrible term: say human, people, or interpersonal skills) are more valuable than technical skills. We are not machines.

Perhaps the greatest HR dysfunction of them all is trying to standardise humans into interchangeable resources. Buckingham[89] taught us long ago to build strengths, not rectify weaknesses. Work with who you've got, maximise their potential, help them to flourish. Build self-organising teams based on skills not roles.

If you hadn't guessed already, our favourite book about the restoration of humanity to work is Hamel and Zanini's *Humanocracy*. Its thesis is that bureaucracy[p186] is the root of work's evils, and the opposite is humanocracy.

The same thing has been said since humans organised; that work doesn't have to be inhuman, that we can create a humanistic[p233] culture at work. It was always the right thing to do. With knowledge workers, it is the only thing to do.

You can't fake this. False humanity is almost worse than a lack. The cynicism is itself poisonous to corporate culture. Amazon recently offered to pay for all staff's college fees. It will be interesting to see how much

---

[88] https://press.careerbuilder.com/2011-08-18-Seventy-One-Percent-of-Employers-Say-They-Value-Emotional-Intelligence-Over-IQ-According-to-CareerBuilder-Survey
[89] Marcus Buckingham, *First Break All the Rules*.

uptake there is. I think this is cynical PR. Many Amazon workers work two jobs, or raise a family. Many work there because they aren't academic. Few will have a hope of going to college. Sometimes I wonder if the cruelty is accidental.

Tokenism is equally counter-productive. Keep your massages and gift certificates until after you've fixed the dysfunctional work system. You don't hand a drowning person a lollipop.

Trust

We must trust people. If we boil all the better ways of working and managing down to one word, it is "trust". It is foundational to all of it: psychological safety, work safety, servant leader, stewardship, empowerment, respect, love. We want to restore trust between individuals, teams, units, and organisations; with customers, between management and workers, with society.

We can build trust in three ways:

1. Deliver results. Do what you said you'd do.
2. Be authentic[p167] and open. Don't lie, don't fake it. Play an open hand, share your thoughts.
3. Trust others. Nobody will trust you as a manager unless you trust them. You don't always have time to earn trust by what you do. You may even have the baggage of things you have done in the past on behalf of an unreasonable work system. Managers and leaders most quickly earn trust by trusting others.

Integrity

In order to achieve the levels of trust necessary for these open ways of working and managing, we must exhibit a personal integrity. The values we espouse and the behaviours we exhibit should align.

The integrity of someone is their ability to be true to their own set of values. We can only judge people against their own value system. Whether we agree with that value system is a different issue. The value system we choose to follow is a matter of morality.

An organisation should conduct itself with integrity, and so should we as individuals. Too many people are driven to compromise their integrity for a paycheck. Try not to do that, it rots you from inside. Stand up when you can. One person can make a difference[90].

Values

Stakeholder capitalism is about our principle of "values over value". When thinking about how to consider or organise these values, it is useful to note that the New Zealand government's Living Standards Framework and the wellbeing focus of government policy recognises a common wealth that is made up of four capitals: ecological, economic, social, and cultural. Organisations must find ways forward that are socially and environmentally sustainable, are ethically sound, that draw all stakeholders together to collaborate, that reflect our common humanity.

---

[90] E.g. Dr. Tadataka Yamada at Glaxo SmithKline https://hbr-org.cdn.ampproject.org/c/s/hbr.org/amp/2019/12/how-one-person-can-change-the-conscience-of-an-organization

We agree with experts[91] that putting too much effort into defining an organisation's values is a waste of time. Skip it altogether, or, if you must, then save messing about by adopting universal values like:

- Honesty
- Respect
- Trust
- Love
- Fairness
- Courage

Or one overarching value like Google's one that they (troublingly) dropped: "don't be evil".

When you define and publish a set of values, they usually end up engendering cynicism when bosses don't walk the walk. You kill them by codifying them. A better approach is to tell stories about yourselves, from the origins and history of the organisation, from which people can infer the values and the expected behaviours. From these stories, we can define a vision of who we aspire to be as an organisation, a common cause or purpose, and the principles that guide our decision making and our work patterns. Those are worth devoting effort to agreeing and describing.

What matters is that we *have* values and principles which we live by, that we live in a principled way, not that we can put them on a motivational poster at work. What you put on the walls are the principles of the way we do things around here, not why. What matters is that we *care* about values, not that we can recite them.

---

[91] https://www.cognitive-edge.com/making-values-mundane-inducing-mendaciousness/

Wholeness

Personal integrity and our striving for inclusion mean that people should be able to bring their whole selves to work, to not have to hang their identity at the door. We should not have to hide those aspects of ourselves which we wish to reveal.

A certain level of caution is called for in unhealthy work cultures. Things we reveal can be used against us or hold us back. How much one reveals is a function of the levels of trust. Trust can only develop and maintained, and be expressed in an environment that is safe. It's a measure of how far we have to go with corporate culture that such caution is necessary.

Nevertheless, the freedom, strength, and relaxation associated with the integrity and honesty of being oneself generally make it worth it. It is a right we should be able to exercise.

Morality[92]

I am venturing outside my own area of expertise - not being a moral philosopher - but it should be clear from the rest of this book that better ways of working depend on advances in thinking, which includes a higher morality than is currently exhibited in many organisations and societies.

Somewhere within Microsoft and other companies, there are programmers who wrote the code to give the NSA their back doors. I guess they rationalised it as sacrificing honesty in the name of national security. They may even have felt good about what they did. Or maybe it

---

[92] What is the difference between morality and ethics? I don't know either. Some say morality is social and ethics is personal. I use them more as morality is from the heart and ethics is from the head.

keeps them awake at night. Perhaps they did it out of fear, pressured to do it and ashamed of having capitulated. I bet the same happens in China.

Even more unsavoury is when games manufacturers change their code to suck up to totalitarian regimes. It is so much easier when it is an unseen foreigner whose freedoms you sell out cheaply.

For the record, I'm not a privacy advocate. This isn't about privacy. And I'm not anti-NSA. We need surveillance, for our protection, to defend our liberty. But we need surveillance with honour, with honesty and transparency, with decency. Clearly that is not what we have been getting, and many IT people made that possible.

More generally we get the society we deserve. We are all faced with ethical(p166) challenges. Sometimes we are asked to do something unethical, and more commonly we see it being done by others. How do you respond to that? How will you respond in future?

Somewhere there are accountants and managers and lawyers who set up Apple's international tax rorts, and similar rorts in a thousand other companies. People go to work every day at tobacco companies, betting shops, casinos, payday loans, and boiler rooms; and millions work inside the military-industrial complex. We may well play a part in activities that go against our personal values, and/or against the interests of our fellow members of society.

We are all victims of the system we are in, and ultimately it is the morality of the system we must change. In the meantime, people suffer to make that change.

The moral position of people working in certain industries is interesting. If they believe they will be on their deathbed contented with what they have done, then at least they must be acting with personal integrity within their own moral framework. I don't think that is always the case: I think some people compromise their own personal values to make a living. That's a shame, as it slowly rots you from within.

Google faced open staff mutiny over their military projects to automate kill target recognition. Edward Snowden is still a hero. So is Chelsea Manning. At some point your morality should matter more than your cool job. It is for all of us to decide where the line is, but it is better to die on your feet than live on your knees. They don't own you[93].

Ethics

If morality is how we feel about a situation, ethics is how we reason about it. As the change in social values accelerates, we must adapt to the moving context and expectations.

...economist Milton Friedman's position on the responsibility of business, the idea that increasing profit within the rules of the game was the sole and righteous goal of executives clearly simplified leadership values and ethics. I suspect that is one less-recognized reason that so many CEOs avidly embraced Friedman's monolithic view for so long. But now as more and more leaders are expanding the scope of their responsibilities and companies are adopting—and compensating leaders on—ESG (environmental, social, and governance) metrics, an increasing number of thorny ethical dilemmas are sure to come along with it[94]

Some of these dilemmas are for the organisation we represent, and its place in society, and some affect us personally, challenging our own

---

[93] http://www.ttjasi.com/
[94] https://www.strategy-business.com/blog/Becoming-a-leader-of-conscience

values. For both types, one way to analyse them is the CLIP framework: consequences, loyalties, identity, and principles[95]. We assess:

- What is the balance of harm?
- What loyalty do we owe others?
- How does this sit with who you are?
- Does this fit our principles?

Authenticity

Be authentic, be your real self. People sense when you are saying or doing things you are not comfortable with. Large organisations are notorious for making managers fake their behaviour or beliefs: they are expected to be a machine of the executive. It creates cynicism and destroys trust, and makes a manager look weak and uncaring. Don't agree to do it and don't make your managers do it.

Some suggest[96] that it is necessary to adopt behaviours that initially feel uncomfortable, even contrived, in order to adapt to a new management role. This is a matter for your own conscience – you might guess that I don't agree.

Vulnerable

Part of authenticity is to be vulnerable. There is no need for bluffing: tell the team how you feel. This is the hardest thing for most of us. It takes more courage to admit you don't know or you are afraid than to pretend otherwise. It is also the greatest builder of trust with your team.

---

[95] *The Conscience Code*, G. Richard Shell (Chair of Wharton School's Legal Studies and Business Ethics)
[96] *The Authenticity Paradox*, HBR, https://hbr.org/2015/01/the-authenticity-paradox

There are limits to when and where we should be exposing our vulnerability. Managers also have a responsibility to protect those watching them. And staff do watch for cues. Finding the nuanced balance is tricky, but worth the effort. We can be open about confusion or concern, and still set an example by explaining how we are working to keep our own emotional stability intact.[97] That's more transparency right there.

"Being vulnerable" is sometimes interpreted to mean exposing our secret selves. Let's be very clear that all it means is a willingness to admit uncertainty or concern in a specific situation, not to indulge in public psychotherapy at work. Inducing people to expose their inner selves is the worst sort of coaching quackery (which HR is riddled with).

Bullshit

Many organizations are drowning in a flood of corporate bullshit, and this is particularly true of organizations in trouble, whose managers tend to make up stuff on the fly and with little regard for future consequences. Bullshitting and lying are not synonymous. While the liar knows the truth and wittingly bends it to suit their purpose, the bullshitter simply does not care about the truth.[98]

There are several forms of bullshit:

- Lies, untruths, distortions, misinformation
- Unsubstantiated beliefs, mysticism/magic, myths, pseudoscience, conspiracy theories
- Authoritarian decree, pulling rank, overruling, suppression

---

[97] https://hbr.org/amp/2019/01/managing-when-the-future-is-unclear
[98] *Confronting indifference toward truth: Dealing with workplace bullshit*, McCarthy et al, Business Horizons, Volume 63, Issue 3, May–June 2020 https://doi.org/10.1016/j.bushor.2020.01.001

- Acronyms and jargon used to obfuscate what is being said

Bullshit is a serious topic of academic research and is effectively a technical term now. There are emerging frameworks for measuring it and for getting rid of it.

We may joke about mushrooms kept in the dark and fed on bullshit, but it is a serious cultural issue. Bullshit induces cynical demotivation, and permission for worse behaviour. It undermines integrity.

Permissioning

Something I learnt from personal relationships is that you give each other permission for certain behaviours. Once one person does something and the other person does not reject that behaviour, then permission is now granted to do it again by either party. When permission is given, it is much harder to take it back. After it is done once, it is difficult to stop doing it again.

So it is at work: once one person bullies or shouts or cheats or harasses, unless it is called out and stopped on that first occurrence then the culture has given permission for it to be done again. People will rationalise the circumstances in which the behaviour is repeated - that there is some special imperative - but it will be repeated. Do not give permission for behaviours which are unacceptable, by tolerating or ignoring them even once. Clearly define and stick to boundaries.

If a behaviour has become permitted, then we need to send a clear message that it is not ok and never was ok. New Zealand is doing a fine job of this with family violence and did it previously with spanking children. At work, most of society has done this with sexual harassment and misogyny. Unfortunately, these behaviours have been given permission in some organisations. It needs to be taken back. Much more widely there is permission for emotional violence: for shouting and bullying and anger. These are not normal acceptable behaviours in any civilised social setting. There is widespread permission for the use of force to coerce people to do that which they don't want to do, that is against their principles. Take it back.

> The culture of any organization is shaped by the worst behavior the leader is willing to tolerate.
>
> - Steve Gruenert and Todd Whitaker

Bad behaviour

The more that we open up our management, the more that conservative people will think that we are increasing the risk of theft and cheating. But of course we get theft and cheating now, so it is not certain that open management will mean more of it or not. It's not as if we are successful in stopping it now. I expect that building a positive open transparent inclusive culture will bring out the best in people and reduce the dysfunctional behaviours not increase them.

But human nature being what it is, we must be ready for when it happens, because it certainly will.

When somebody steals or lies or cheats or bullies or some other unacceptable behaviour, we must not react by introducing controls and reducing trust for everyone. We must learn from what happened.

What was it that made that person feel entitled to do that? Was there something about the culture that made them feel it was ok? How can we change that so that people do not feel they have permission for bad behaviour?

What was it about the system that allowed them to get away with it? What can we change to prevent it in future without putting an extra burden on honest work?

Nine times out of ten, a failure is a function of the system, not the individual. So do not assume malice when usually it is an honest mistake.

In the small number of times when it really is a dysfunctional person, then performance management must be taken offline outside the work. Do not introduce controls or tests that get in the way of honest people getting their jobs done. Deal with dysfunctional behaviour outside the work asynchronously, so that honest work does not get slowed down.

If we always focus on the negative, on the things that go wrong, then we will develop attitudes of suspicion and cynicism, and we will go back to distrust and control. If we focus on the positives, on all the times that people rewarded our trust with loyalty and excellence, then we will continue to build on that, to grow a more successful open organisation.

You have to trust people even when you know for sure that at some point somebody is going to betray that trust. This is true in life and in work. You cannot function effectively if you distrust everyone. The paranoia kills you and it stops everything. We must trust people and then deal with the exceptions.

Diversity

Diversity is an essential element for creative thought, innovation, and – especially important right now – adaptability for survival. The fastest path to that diversity of thought is to ensure people with a diversity of origin have access to work at our organisation. This means removing systemic and unconscious bias from recruiting, retention, and advancement; and creating an organisation that a diverse range of people would want to work at.

The obvious examples are supporting immigrant non-citizens to get visas, normalising gender diversity, removing bro culture so that women can feel safe, actively recruiting the neurodiverse, and confronting racism in the workplace. A group of exclusively white cis men is always going to be less diverse in thinking. It will take much harder work to achieve and maintain any range of ideas than a heterogenous group.

Diversity makes work better:

- It is more fun, more colourful, which boosts staff retention.
- It is more creative, which increases innovation.
- It is more insightful, which aids problem solving.

> "In strategy making, you have to diverge—a lot—before you converge. This requires a process that encourages radical thinking and includes new voices. Strategy making should be a companywide conversation that is open to employees, customers, and external partners."
>
> – Gary Hamel, Michele Zanini

Inclusion

"Diversity is a fact; inclusion is an act." To reap the benefits of diversity, it's not enough to have a mix of people, to simply stop excluding some. We must welcome and embrace diversity as something we all want, we all value.

The measure of this is that all people feel welcome in the workplace, and feel included in the work. They feel safe[p174].

"Cultural fit" is a hot topic as I write this. It is one of the hardest dilemmas in organisational culture. You want people who fit in, and at the same time you want diversity. There may be definitions that accommodate both, but it is tricky. Better to recruit for "cultural add"[99], not "cultural fit".

(This is Teal Unicorn's mascot, Uníc, drawn by Seharuu Nguyen)

In a culturally diverse organisation, some people are not going to fit in, e.g. racists, sexists, religious or political extremists. All sorts of views that do not embrace diversity will not work in a diverse work culture. They may have a place in social culture (though not at my place) but work is different. We have to all get along and collaborate.

Work is political now. You don't have to hang up your identity at the door when you start work anymore. People have a right to be their whole self[(p164)]. And some whole selves do not fit together. So, paradoxically, a work culture that embraces diversity, necessarily has to be slightly less diverse.

---

[99] https://www.fastcompany.com/90358626/culture-fit-vs-culture-add

Psychological Safety [100]

Psychological safety is not about being nice and agreeing all the time. It is about feeling safe to speak up or disagree in a civilised manner without rebuke or retribution. At its extreme, it is about feeling safe to be a whistle-blower.

Psychological safety provides the right environment for receiving candid feedback, admitting mistakes, and learning from your colleagues.
- *Gustavo Razzetti*[101]

There are four levels of safety[102], where people feel:
1. included
2. safe to learn
3. safe to contribute
4. safe to challenge

Organisations can only be healthy when people feel safe to be transparent, honest, vulnerable, and direct, i.e. open. In particular, safety is important to harvest the value from failure by allowing people to be open about it.

We want to get to that highest level. We must create not just safe spaces but "brave spaces"[103] where we are not afraid of confrontation. We do this by creating a culture of inclusion, diversity of thought, and freedom to experiment.

Friends can disagree and still be friends (within limits). A safe workplace is a friendly workplace.

---

[100] The leading writer on psychological safety is Amy Edmondson of Harvard, who coined the term.
[101] https://www.fearlessculture.design/blog-posts/the-psychological-safety-ladder-canvas
[102] *The 4 Stages of Psychological Safety*, Timothy R. Clark
[103] *The Art of Effective Facilitation: Reflections From Social Justice Educators*, Arao and Clemens, 2013

Human Resilience

Resilience is the ability to bend in the face of a challenge, even break under it, and then bounce back. This is true of systems and of people, in groups and as individuals.

The key to mental resilience seems to be optimism[104]. We can build a culture of optimism at work: supporting each other positively, celebrating advances, responding constructively to events.

This description of recovering from trauma seems applicable to coming back from major failure at work:

Creating a narrative in which the trauma is seen as a fork in the road that enhances the appreciation of paradox - loss and gain, grief and gratitude, vulnerability and strength. A manager might compare this to what the leadership studies pioneer Warren Bennis called "crucibles of leadership." The narrative specifies what personal strengths were called upon, how some relationships improved, how spiritual life strengthened, how life itself was better appreciated, or what new doors opened.
- Martin Seligman

Recently, Marcus Buckingham did what he does, identifying ten statements about work which correlate with mental resilience[105]. They point to clear leadership, empowerment, and motivation.

---

[104] https://hbr.org/2011/04/building-resilience
[105] https://www.adpri.org/wp-content/uploads/2020/10/18231304/The-Sources-of-Resilience.pdf

Respect

Only labour can be standardised and measured, and managed by numbers. Knowledge work can't: diversity is essential, work is intangible. Which is beside the point: that's not how we should treat anyone. Everybody deserves to be treated with dignity and respect. They're not "human resources", they're people, colleagues, friends.

This means not forcing people to do things against their will. Too many employers use the fact that they are paying people as an excuse to use force. This includes how we treat people who are terminated(p205), or who resign: everybody else is watching. As I said, force works on those you can measure, but badly: it creates resentment, cynicism, even outright resistance and subversion. It certainly doesn't create loyalty, motivation, respect, or community. And it doesn't work at all on knowledge workers.

Moving into a management position doesn't suddenly make somebody superior, and it certainly doesn't make them smarter or more knowledgeable. We are all peers, colleagues, collaborators in the organisation's success. Everybody deserves equal respect.

Fun

There is no reason work can't be fun. It's fun to do hard work when you do it together, with camaraderie. It's fun to fail, when you have a laugh, recover well, and come back stronger. And of course, it's fun to succeed, to win, to get the result. Work should be full of games, of play, of shared merriment. Lighten up, win the game not the war. Don't make fun compulsory. Don't make it a cult of happiness. There should be variety: seriousness, sadness, tension, even anger when we can't stop ourselves (but it's not ok - don't give permission(p169)). All emotion is normal. Let's strive to make fun the dominant one.

Love

The hippies may not have got a lot right, but normalising peace and love as aspirations was a gift to future generations.

In English the word love is not limited to a couple falling in love. It has the meanings of love for your group, your community, for humanity, for the planet. You can love anything. Let's stop being squeamish about using the word at work. Let's work with our hearts as well as our minds. Let's talk about love.

Once we love our workmates, we treat colleagues like comrades, not resources. When we love our customers, we act with integrity in their best interests. Because we love society, we rebel at attempts to use the organisation to harm it.

In early 2020 Rob had cancer and was not able to go to Vietnam, so Cherry went alone. I have a game called The Message[106] where participants build a large message on the wall out of sticky notes. When our students heard why Rob hadn't come, this was the message they decided to create:

---

[106] https://tealunicorn.com/message

Systems thinking

A system is a bunch of things that are connected to each other. It has some boundary we draw around it, and what is outside is its environment. Real-world systems are also connected to their environment, very few are "closed". So the boundary line can be somewhat arbitrary - it's a mental construct not an actual thing (which makes security that obsesses with the perimeter look pretty silly). Systems thinking, or systems theory, tries to understand how they behave as a whole, as an entity. Systems often have emergent behaviours - they arise from the interaction of the parts, not from any one part. Systems are the product of their interactions not the sum of their behaviours[107], so they get complex quickly with increasing complicatedness. They are all VUCA(p245). We only pretend they are simple and predictable. At a moment in time, we might constrain them into a simpler situation.

Systems thinking is a huge body of knowledge that I can only point you to, but there are a few aspects that we discuss in this book. We look at some of the aspects specifically of systems of work here, and later in the book, we look at the general idea of complexity(p241).

Thinking of work as a system (of nested systems) is one leg of our Human Systems Adaptability(p159) definition of better ways of working. The ideas have been around for over a century, and they are becoming increasingly prominent at work, especially since the ideas of complexity emerged in recent decades.

---

[107] Russell Ackoff, in this video https://youtu.be/aoooqJ-pOH4

Self-organising teams

A team of people is a system. To truly be a team, they must have strong relationships. A team works together. If they don't, they're just a group of people. You are unlikely to ever find a functioning team of more than ten people. That's why almost all sports teams are no more than ten (rugby is two teams; baseball and basketball are collaborating individuals more than cohesive teams).

Many teams of adults are quite capable of organising themselves. As we become more humanistic, we empower staff and flip the hierarchy[p211]. Increasingly we should give the team the goals and the work, and leave them to get on with it. They can work out who does what, and when; what they are going to do; and what else they may need. The more they organise themselves, the more engaged they'll be in the outcomes.

Environment

I am a great believer in the importance of the physical aspects of work. Our physical work environment has a major impact on our productivity. Here are some aspects:

Workplace

I had my own office as recently as 2005, but most of the time we work in open-plan offices or cubicles. Some people thrive on the energy of many people working around them, and others can't cope with it at all. We must make space for neurodiversity to maximise value from our workforce.

Research[108] suggests the most productive workplaces are those that provide a mix of private and public spaces, large and small, with fluidity so that we can organise the work around the space and the space around the work. Fluidity means we can reorganize the layout and we can reorganize which spaces belong to which groups and teams.

An essential part of a team having space that belongs to them is the ability to make their mark on it. There is a fashion amongst architects and facilities managers that office space should be as sterile as a laboratory. Security policy sometimes tries to do the same. This is psychopathic: it dehumanises the space and guarantees diminished performance. Workspace should be personal and colourful: marked and branded by those who work within it, to make it their own. We discuss the importance of information radiators on walls elsewhere, but information on walls also serves to make them colourful and distinctive to the team.

Healthy office

Modern office buildings are hermetically sealed and climate controlled. We are increasingly coming to understand the importance of fresh air. Many office environments are unhealthy with high levels of CO_2, particulates, evaporating chemicals, bacteria, and viruses, bad light temperature and flicker, and static charges. I originally wrote this before COVID-19. The research that has come out of that has absolutely nailed the harm of closed-air environments.

I have heard the excuse that all plants and animals are banned from an office building because of the risk that somebody might be allergic to them. This is clearly hypocritical in a building where you can't even open the windows. The benefits of a more natural environment with plants and

---

[108] E.g https://journals.plos.org/plosone/article?id=10.1371/journal.pone.0232943

animals present far exceeds any negative impact on a small number of people.

The fashion for introducing fruit, massage, and exercise to work environments is to be applauded, but there is much more that we can do to make it a healthy environment.

Remote work

Much has been said about remote work since the onset of the COVID-19 pandemic. Here, we define remote work as where some or all of the team are connecting to each other virtually rather than being physically co-located. Somebody suggested to me that remote work should be defined as when you work away from home, which I quite like as an inversion. Or I have seen WFH defined as "work from here", as in wherever I happen to be at this moment.

Seen through an Open Work lens, remote working should be decided by the self-organising team collaboratively. The team needs to find the balance of meeting the needs of the team for optimum performance and optimum well-being of the individuals.

I think it would be unusual for a team to work 100% remotely. Given the needs of the lizard brain[p237] to "share air" at least occasionally, it would be a rare team if it did not need to come together on some cadence, whether weekly or annually. In fact I suggest that a team that works 100% remotely isn't really a team, it is a group of individuals sharing work. It will never be as effective as a true team, producing joint work maximising the potential of all the members. When 100% remote does work well, I suggest that it reflects on the introverted nature of the members of the team, and perhaps that their work has low coupling. It is unlikely to be optimal for most cases.

Equally, forcing people to always work in a physically co-located office is seldom likely to be optimal. Many people, including me, get very little done in a crowded environment.

So, in most cases, a hybrid approach is going to be best to allow staff to work remotely when it suits them, yet the team also agreeing times when they will come together. The proportion of each will be all over the spectrum from all remote to all co-located, depending on the team.

Value network

We might model the world with simplified models of a flow like a stream, or perhaps a complicated interwoven flow like a braided river, but the reality is invariably that the flow - work, information, influence, or value, whatever we are observing - flows in all directions in an intertwined network like the water flowing through a swamp or wetland. Sometimes the overall direction can be hard to discern. In many instances we co-create, in bi-directional relationships.

Value stream

In order to use some of the best-known work-optimisation methods, we need to be able to describe a process as a flow of work, with inputs being turned by a transaction - a series of processes - into outputs. This is a value stream.

That only happens in highly bounded linear flows, where the simplistic deterministic approximation is close enough, and only so long as the system remains well behaved within its bounds.

This allows the flow to be defined and repeatable, so that we can measure multiple transactions to get statistical information for improvement, and so that we can automate. No matter how much they try to make it otherwise, the flow models of Lean, Lean Six Sigma, Theory of Constraints, Business Process Reengineering, and many others, really only work for a simple linear flow. Within that context, the thinking is useful. I use Value Stream Mapping whenever I can.

This approximation is only possible when we zoom in close on a value network. When we step back, the linear bit of the system is invariably embedded in a more complicated network.

Planning

> **Charles Lambdin**
> @CGLambdin
>
> Traditional planning is sort of like planning out all your moves in a game of chess while it's still the opening.
>
> 10:05 am · 21 Mar 21 · Twitter for iPhone

Conventional planning is most often based on a simple linear model of "Define once, execute as close to perfectly as we can, and then measure against the definition". Once we are into execution, there is often little or no opportunity to modify the plan. Or there might be a fixed margin for uncertainty, which is sometimes waste and sometimes not enough.

Such planning is better for tangible physical projects within known engineering domains. Projects have a terrible track record for abstract intangible knowledge work. It is a reasonable approximation to treat a bridge or building as a simple system, where everything can be defined upfront. Even the variations are highly predictable. We have no choice anyway, because we can only execute once on physical objects.

Most knowledge work is not like this. We are creating intangible, generally digital, objects which can be recreated many times at relatively lower costs. Iteration and increment are not only possible but relatively easy. With intangibles, such as software, we can iterate and increment - i.e. we can be agile(p223) - which yields better results at less risk than define-once-execute-perfectly. Increasingly in modern project management thinking, there are mechanisms to try to be as incremental, resilient, and adaptable as possible even with concrete objects.

This enables agile planning, which is how we would like to do all planning if we could, because the world is VUCA(p245): even before we start, our information is imperfect, rendering some of our assumptions wrong; and then before we have finished a piece of work, the circumstances and information have changed.

Therefore, we should plan only enough to execute another iteration to create another increment and discover new information. Any more planning than that is arguably waste.

There is even a school of thought that no-plan-at-all is optimal. Optimise to the current state, to explore the space. Don't plan past now. No matter where the world goes, we will track as near as we could have to the best possible state at all times. It is intuitively uncomfortable, but I struggle to fault the logic.

You don't have to take such an extreme position on planning to realise that lots of planning is theatre to create the illusion that we know what we are doing, usually to reassure someone sufficiently that they will give us money.

Bureaucracy

Bureaucracy is the idea that if we formalise policy, we can be impartial in how we administer it to create the fairest possible system. In principle, this is the most democratic and just way to run an organisation or society. In practice, it dehumanises it. Policy is always too simplistic for the real world. It is always an approximation which fails to account for the complexity of humanity. Individuals get hurt in the blind machine.

This is a polarity tension. There is no reasonable way to reconcile the dilemma between impartial justice and empathetic caring.

Bureaucracy is an unfortunate necessity which we can optimise for.[109] It must be accompanied by mitigating mechanisms that introduce humanity to work. This is an area the authors are still exploring. I welcome any suggestions. Here is some good advice:

There are three things we must do to eliminate bureaucracy's Kafkaesque aspects. We must make it lean by removing waste and shrinking lead times. We must make it capable of learning; that is, changing as the environment changes and as better ways are found to accomplish goals. And we must make it enabling—that is, helpful as a way to get things done rather than a no-saying, gatekeeping, troll-controlled impediment.[110]

---

[109] For example, see Mark Schwatz's new book *The Art of Bureaucracy* which is self-indulgently intellectual but makes some good points.
[110] https://itrevolution.com/how-to-fix-bureaucracy/

Adaptability

I have seen this idea a few times:

Adaptability = Agility[p223] + Resilience[p192]

An organisation ready to adapt to changing circumstances needs the agility to change quickly enough to take advantage; and the resilience to survive the inevitable impacts, setbacks, and J-curves[p189].

Adaptability is more important than efficiency in a VUCA world. Both agility and resilience cost money. Surviving and thriving doesn't come for free.

For example, the COVID lockdowns in 2020 exposed how vulnerable global supply chains are. Just In Time manufacturing is a fragile system. We should learn that inventory is not always waste. Systems need buffer stocks to cope with variability, to give the system resilience.

As another example, instead of conventional planning I recommend[111] preparing multiple options to respond to potential future scenarios, some of which will never be used. This can be seen as wasteful.

As another example, we have seen how agility involves continuous iterative experimentation, and how experiments often result in failure. We will abandon some investments, throw work away. This is an inevitable result of finding our way.

Agility also requires greater headroom, more slack capacity. The principles of agility are often perceived to be not efficient.

---

[111] https://tealunicorn.com/st-with-new-ways-of-planning/

Fluidity

In a VUCA world we must be constantly adapting. Fixed structures act against us. We must make as many aspects of the work as fluid as we possibly can. For example:

- Work passes freely between teams. Value streams[p183] can switch to different paths as necessary.
- The formal organisational structure changes often and incrementally to track how people are working together.
- People change their role whenever work demands, based on their skills, or they have no designated roles at all. They swarm to what needs to be done.
- Teams assemble themselves as needed and people move between teams.
- Money can be reallocated quickly to fund changing patterns of work.
- Technology and processes can be reconfigured quickly.

Failure

All work systems are complex systems. The future is unknowable. Even the current state is unknowable. Therefore, we don't know the outcome of work until we do something. All work is experiment. Experiments fail. Therefore, failure is a normal part of work.

There is no wrong way, because all experiment includes failure, and all failure has value as learning.

> "The only real failure is failure to learn from failure"
>
> - Henry Ford, perhaps, near enough.

Mistakes - human errors - are still valuable failure. We take responsibility for our mistakes and learn how not to do that again. But more importantly we share that learning or play a role in a bigger learning exercise, and identify options for the next experiment, so that nobody else has to make that mistake again. We do it by examining why we made that mistake: What pressure were we under? What in the system led us to the decisions we made? What distractions? What poka yoke should there be? ...

The key is the psychological safety to share our experience and our ideas, not hide them. It's a matter of professionalism that our mistake hurts us. It's a matter of safety that nobody else does. Punishing failure destroys its value, transforming it from an asset to a cost.

If failure is embraced as new value – even embracing incompetent failure – then it will be presented in the open for the value to be extracted. Nobody goes to work to deliberately screw up. Something in the system makes it happen. Fix the system. Failure becomes an asset instead of an (often hidden) cost.

Failure is inevitable. Make it acceptable, normal, welcome even. All failure is an advance but only if you let it be one.

Then the next discussion is how the value is only realised if you have a learning organisation with a continual improvement machine to realise the value. This reduces future failure.

The J-curve

Whenever we make a change to how we work (or manage), there is the J-curve. Understanding it and managing it is a great aid to minimising risk and advancing well in a VUCA world.

Every change to a working system will have an initial negative impact on performance until we can identify issues, fix problems, learn new processes, and start to optimise performance of the new system. New teams need to form before they can perform. Every time we change anything about how we work, the performance of the work system goes backwards before it goes forwards.

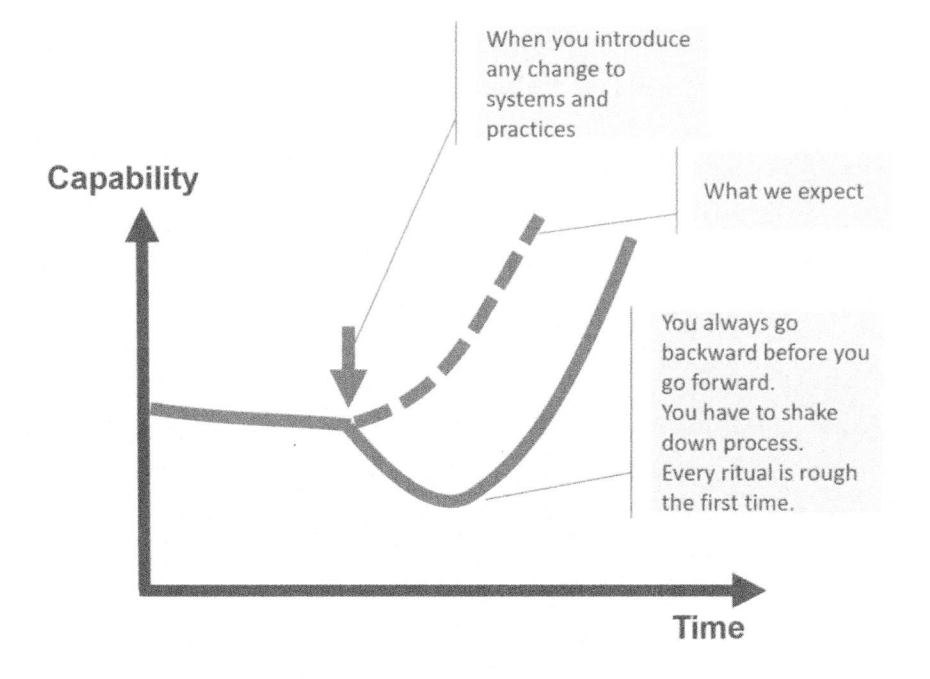

Capability (y-axis) vs **Time** (x-axis)

- When you introduce any change to systems and practices
- What we expect
- You always go backward before you go forward. You have to shake down process. Every ritual is rough the first time.

This is not "failure". This is a law of nature, for at least four reasons:

- People need to practice the new way, to get the hang of it. My rule of thumb is: all new activities take at least three iterations before they start to work well.
- It's a complex system. We don't know what the effect of changes will be until we try them. Nobody knows. It's all an experiment.
- We get it wrong. We make mistakes, inevitably - nobody is perfect.
- People may be actively resistant, disengaged, or at least holding back to see how it goes.

An observer can take a short-term view of a J-curve and say it was all bad. Or take a longer-term view and look for the up-turn. Management must not lose their nerve.

Imperfection

If we worried less about perfection or ideological purity, and accepted more about the imperfect muck of human endeavour, we could all get on with making work better.

If you drop the finest purest essence into a bucket of dirty water it will improve the bucket but dilute and sully the essence. So it is with all our ideas and aspirations. The world is better, the ideal is compromised. Embrace it. Progress can only be measured from where you have come. Comparisons against an ideal future are pointless, demoralising, exclusionary, elitist, and contrary to the ethos of these better ways.

Work Safety

The safety sector (medical, aviation, engineering, industrial...) is undergoing a transformation analogous to the general shift to agile, open ways of working. The parallels become apparent when you study both.

It goes by various names such as Safety II, Safety Differently, or High Reliability Organisations, and links to growing areas of study around Resilience Engineering and Human Factors.

The new safety thinking is influential on how we think about better ways of working and managing. The best place to start is the video *Safety Differently - the Movie*, available on YouTube.

I sum it up as two flips:

- from focusing on stopping what went wrong in the past, to increasing what goes right in the future.

- from people are the problem and systems the solution, to systems are the problem and people are the solution.

Hopefully, the crossovers to what we discuss here are evident: trust, blamelessness, embrace of failure, psychological safety, resilience, learning, continual improvement, openness.

Resilience

Resilience can mean[112]:

> 1 rebound: "rebounds from disrupting or traumatic events and returns to previous or normal activities"
>
> 2 robustness: "is able to manage increasing complexity, stressors, and challenge"
>
> 3 graceful extensibility: "extends performance, or brings extra adaptive capacity to bear, when surprise events challenge its boundaries"
>
> 4 sustained adaptability: "is able to adapt to future surprises as conditions continue to evolve"

Resilience is the ability to come back from setbacks and grow from the experience, in other words organisational antifragility. (Antifragile is an awesome new concept that we don't have room to cover here. Learn about it.)

---

[112] *Four concepts for resilience and the implications for the future of resilience engineering*, D.D. Woods, Safety Science.

Resilience engineering is building work systems to be resilient: ensuring that our people and systems cope, recover, and grow stronger when things go wrong.

Business resilience is less commonly described. It refers to:
- the resilience of our business systems to survive stress, to heal, to recover, and to grow stronger as a result (antifragile) by learning with intention. Get organised: be ready for anything that happens now, be prepared. Assume it will go wrong. Expect human error. Expect Black Swans. Expect catastrophe. Make systems fail safe, self-healing, evolutionary, anything to better survive failures. Stop:
    - building fragile systems that only work when everything goes right.
    - ...especially "Tarzan" systems that let you swing out into space on the assumption that the next vine is there.
    - optimising all the buffers out in the name of JIT efficiency.
    - optimising all the capacity out in the name of utilisation.
    - dragging legacy debt along in the name of ROI or sunk cost.
    - expecting humans to get it right every time.
- the resilience of our people to cope with adversity, to have: reserves of capacity and energy to deal with the unplanned; positive attitudes and morale; optimism; a sense of strength and capability.
- the resilience of our culture which embraces adversity as growth, challenge as opportunity, failure as normal learning, and destruction as a refresh.

Open Management

The core premise of my work at Teal Unicorn is that people can't work in better ways until you *manage* in better ways.

> Some people formally embrace the agile way of working but do not let go of their existing organizational structure and governance. That defeats the whole purpose and only creates more frustration.
>
> – Peter Jacobs, ING Netherlands CIO

The goal of this book is to promote those better ways: **"Open Management", that is invitational, transparent, humane, and subordinate to work.**

In the same way that I characterised better ways of working as Human Systems Adaptability[p159], maybe I can characterise better ways of managing as Inviting Organising Service. I think those are the three main headings for better management, though I'm still shaking that down, my thinking is immature. Send feedback.

- Inviting: creating an environment for the humanistic ways of working
- Organising: creating the conditions for work systems to perform well
- Service: providing support for those doing the work

In this book, the definition of **a manager is one who uses the authority given to them to manage the resources made available to them and the people working with them to organise outcomes asked of them**. (Back in Part One, I defined three kinds of managers: work, personnel, and executive).

This book is about improving management, not eliminating management. We will always need somebody who accepts a goal from the organisation, and has authorisation to organise the organisation to achieve it. They will take responsibility for developing people, or resources of the organisation, or functions and processes, or the delivery of work. That's management, even if it may look wildly different in future. It may not be a job position, or even a role that people adopt, but it is an activity that will happen.

> You might infer that managers are less important in a meritocracy than in a hierarchical organization because they make fewer direct decisions. Nothing could be further from the truth. Our managers play a vital role in **building, supporting, and moderating** the meritocracy.
>
> - Jim Whitehurst (my emphasis)

I like to say "good managers play golf". Or whatever pastime, because...

- management is about thinking.
- you should set an example of self-care.
- you shouldn't need to be there all the time.
- you should show that staff are empowered.
- you must get out of the way.

Middle managers

We will always need somebody observing the work, close to it, with time for thinking about better ways, and coming up with solutions to challenges. Right now, that's the middle managers: they are the often-unsung engine of innovation in most organisations. Maybe their role will be performed by coaches and scrum-masters in future, but that could still be called management. In one study[113], 80% of the 117 separate projects initiated by senior management had failed or had fallen short of expectations. In contrast, 80% of those initiated by middle managers had succeeded:

Middle managers make valuable contributions to the realization of radical change at a company—contributions that go largely unrecognized by most senior executives. These contributions occur in four major areas. First, middle managers often have value-adding entrepreneurial ideas that they are able and willing to realize—if only they can get a hearing. Second, they're far better than most senior executives are at leveraging the informal networks at a company that make substantive, lasting change possible. Third, they stay attuned to employees' moods and emotional needs, thereby ensuring that the change initiative's momentum is maintained. And finally, they manage the tension between continuity and change—they keep the organization from falling into extreme inertia, on the one hand, or extreme chaos, on the other.

Managerial resistance

Conversely, middle managers are the epicentre of our challenges in advancing to better ways of working and managing. They are the foot soldiers of the organisational "immune system", the metaphorical T-cells, that react against internal irritants such as change agents, to smother them, shut them down, expel them. Most consultants such as the authors have been ejected from an organisation by such a process at some point in our careers.

---

[113] *In Praise of Middle Managers*, Quy Huy, HBR, https://hbr.org/2001/09/in-praise-of-middle-managers

It is important to understand that such people are only doing their job, as they see it. Middle managers are often long-serving employees, loyal to the system they helped create. Many of their goals and KPIs are focused on controlling risk and keeping the system within current bounds: that's what they are there for, that's their purpose, that's how they are measured.

Moreover, middle managers tend to naturally be risk averse. If they are risk tolerant, they tend to keep rising up the hierarchy. The risk averse dig in.

Finally, the cynical would say most middle managers rose to the level of their own incompetence. The smart ones move up or out. The less smart ones stay. We try not to be pejorative. Managers are as much victims of the system they help perpetuate as the others working in it.

Managers who resist change, who act as the immune system, are (mostly) not doing it out of ill will. They are acting with the best intentions, to do what they believe they are supposed to, to protect the organisation from threats to its proper functioning.

> It is difficult to get a man to understand something, when his salary depends upon his not understanding it.
>
> - Upton Jennings

Scientific management

Scientific Management sees the organisation of people as a technical problem to be solved by science and data. Humans are component resources that are selected, placed, and shaped to optimise outcomes. Also known as Taylorism, it is a way to manage people who do defined repeatable work (agricultural, industrial, clerical) - what I call "transactional" - where we regard those people as fungible replaceable resources, and where the goal of management is to maximise the value to shareholders from the employee asset. Or "human capital stock", as economists so lovingly put it.

Such management has come up short when managing knowledge workers, those who do non-transactional work (inventing, designing, building, solving, healing…). You can't see what they do, you can't unravel the work of the individual from the team, and you can't measure quality without enormous costs. So you can't make knowledge workers do anything.

Measurement

Peter Drucker is often quoted as saying "if you can't measure it you can't improve it" or "…manage it". He didn't say it[114]. Nor did Deming[115]. Nor would they. It is nonsense. Any manager who is incapable without metrics is a terrible manager. You can drive a car without a dashboard. Anyone who is incapable of making improvements without numbers hasn't danced with the system(p246).

> What gets measured gets managed - even when it's pointless to measure and manage it, and even if it harms the purpose of the organisation to do so.
>
> - Peter Drucker

How can improvement not be obvious? If we improved, how can we not tell the system is better? It is usually obvious what needs improving, how

---

[114] https://www.drucker.institute/thedx/measurement-myopia/
[115] https://deming.org/myth-if-you-cant-measure-it-you-cant-manage-it/

to improve it, and whether it has improved, to anyone immersed in the work. The problem, need, or risk is observable, it doesn't need instrumentation to metricate it. If we are getting more done and delivering more value, we can see that. It was easy to see everywhere I worked. Three quotes from three different clients:

> "I finally get it. I noticed there is so much more laughter in meetings".
>
> "I left 6 months ago and I don't recognise this place".
>
> "You can see the difference just walking around".

The solution is generally not as obvious. That's an entirely different thing. It has no need for instrumentation either. We can experiment with ideas to see their effect on entirely observable phenomena we are trying to change. We explore the domain, probing our way into the dark.

There is one special case: for incremental optimisation of a bounded flow, instrumentation is necessary. We must measure statistical information about the transactions, to discern significance of the variability, to know whether we have in fact improved. This refers to e.g. process control, CMMI, Value Stream Mapping, or Lean Six Sigma.

For managing a bunch of people interacting to produce a pseudo-organic complex adaptive entity called an organisation, not so much. Measurement is only a guide, which can be misleading as often as useful. Or actively harmful: all metrics distort behaviour. People optimise to the measure, not to the underlying goal.

You either embrace complexity and build capability, or pretend it's simple (and introduce things like KPIs). Life just doesn't work like that.

- Simon Wardley

Even the domain of economics has recognized that pure analytics don't describe the world well, and has expanded its view to include the human aspects of behavioural economics.

By all means have KPIs and other metrics but don't manage by them. Use them only as indicators, it is in the name. Numbers tell you when agility is needed: that you need to change what you're doing.

> **White Owl** @white_owly
>
> I have torn up a lot of metrics because the shadows they cast were larger than the light they let in.
>
> 11:51 am · 13 Jul 19 · Twitter Web App

Measuring people

> Tell me how you measure me, and I will tell you how I will behave.
>
> - Eliyahu M. Goldratt
>
> People with targets and jobs dependent upon meeting them will probably meet the targets – even if they have to destroy the enterprise to do it.
>
> - possibly W. Edwards Deming

It is impossible to measure a human being fairly. To even try is to treat humans as machines.

Psychological profiling is corporate astrology. It can be an amusing team building exercise, for the conversations it triggers, but should never be used to assess people, before or after hiring. Profiling is often required for job applicants, even internal ones going for a new role. And people are rejected on the basis of it. It is also used to shape professional development plans, and even used sometimes to put teams together. Given that none of it has any scientific basis beyond the opinions of psychiatrists based on the hypotheses of Jung, that's unreasonable treatment.

This is not just a personal opinion, but one shared by many. I haven't researched the field, so I'm not equipped or interested in evidential debate. (I do know enough to know that most tools are Jungian, including the widely discredited Myers-Briggs MBTI).

In fact, this is like most fields of knowledge these days: it is too complicated now for laypersons to study. We need to observe expert consensus, experts being those who spend decades getting doctorates and immersing full-time in real research.

You can't use numbers either to judge humans. The explanation is always too complex. Numbers are dehumanising. Humans don't lend themselves to measurement.

Even deeper, I have an ideological objection to measuring people, unless they choose to go and get themselves measured as part of their personal journey. Using numbers on people is not how we should treat colleagues.

If we cannot measure humans, how do we assess people? With human judgement, not numbers and not machines. We should choose carefully who gets to do that, to ensure justice. If anybody gets to judge their colleagues, it should be someone as close as possible to that person. And preferably multiple people. In other words, their teammates. The further someone is from that person, the less right they have to be judging, assessing, or measuring them. Looking at you, HR.

Second best is their direct manager, especially if they have had a long-term relationship. This is yet another reason to separate people management from work management. Work structures may change often, but let's keep people structures stable so that personnel managers get to know their people.

> "because knowledge work cannot be measured the way manual work can, one cannot tell a knowledge worker in a few simple words whether he is doing the right job and how well he is doing it"
>
> - Peter Drucker

Performance

Nobody sets out to fail. If we learn and improve, we are doing our best and that deserves respect.

A weed is just a plant in the wrong place. A people manager's job is to help employees find the right place. Occasionally that place is outside the organisation, but usually not. If someone is failing to perform, that reflects as much on their manager (and the work system) as on themselves. A manager's job is to work with what they've got.

Pressure

Machismo is misplaced in the workplace. It is not war.

This message went around social media recently:
Grapes must be crushed to make wine
Diamonds form under pressure
Olives are pressed to release oil
Seeds grow in darkness
Whenever you feel crushed, under pressure, pressed, or in darkness, you're in a powerful place of transformation.
TRUST THE PROCESS

This is a dangerously bad message, patronising and lacking in humanity. It is management gaslighting.

"The grape or olive is completely and utterly destroyed in the process, and the benefit is not for the grape or olive but for the consumer of their remains. This is the myth of self-sacrificial servitude"[116].

Nobody has the right to crush anyone else, least of all in the belief that it is for their own good. People may choose to take hard decisions. That's nothing like having pressure imposed on you at work. Nobody has the right to abuse others in the name of work. People aren't grapes or olives or seeds. Nobody should be treating them like objects to be shaped or processed. They get to "process" themselves, voluntarily, in their own way. It is basic human rights, not to mention love and respect.

If you accept that bad advice, that's a victim mentality. If you don't know why you are working hard, and if you are not consciously opting in, and if you aren't satisfied by it, then that's abuse.

Punishment

Anyone who thinks they have the right to punish grown adults needs help.

The exception is the military, where a critical success factor is to modify the beliefs and culture to the point where humans are ready to kill other humans. Punishment is necessary to induce such behaviour in people, to dehumanise them.

The other exception is unacceptable behaviour. People who act outside the laws of society should be referred to the police. It shouldn't be hidden in-house.

---

[116] https://twitter.com/AlexBThomson/status/1393853127707828234

People who act legally but outside the values of society or the organisation, should be dealt with by performance management (not within the work). Even here, "punishment" is an unhealthy word. There should be consequences. There should be open conversation about disappointment not anger, and opportunities for redemption. (See also "Firing", next page)

That is not what we are concerned about here. We are referring to a culture of punishing low performance[p203] or failure[p188].

Punitive culture has to end. This is front of mind with all the armchair COVID critics calling for civil servant resignations – troublingly the most vocal are bosses. How they think those dealing with COVID will work better with powerful people calling for their scalps is beyond me.

The value in failures is what we can learn from them. If failure is punished, it only drives future behaviour underground. It will get buried, where you have to dig for any value, and often never even know it is there. When it is buried, the only impacts are the costs. And nobody works well when they are governed by fear. Punitive cultures only create more mistakes in future.

Another discussion is how punitive culture harms morale and engagement, which damages productivity, lowers quality, and increases errors, ensuring more future failures.

A final line of enquiry from here is how to free ourselves from punitive culture. That's what Open Management is all about.

Firing

Firing people should always be a last resort, not an instrument of change.

If you rely on firings to achieve change, sure you will get there faster but a lot of those you keep will never forgive you. You generate cultural debt. Humans are animals, we have lizard brains(p237). We need safety and security to be productive. You will never get good work out of people in a state of fear. And you will never get loyalty out of people when you have already exhibited your lack of loyalty to some of their colleagues. Firing people is a blunt instrument, violence which traumatises those who remain. It is not a positive cultural tool. You better be sure that everybody you want to stay agrees with a firing decision.

How often are those you fire genuinely malevolent, and how often are they actually acting with good intentions? Even the malevolent ones, what makes them like that?

Stop making it about the individuals. Fix the system. The majority come around - people blossom once you get the work system off their back.

If you must treat people as "human resources", then don't waste the resource: skills, talent, relationships, training investment, institutional knowledge, familiarity with systems. All of these are assets that it costs money to replace. Not to mention the cost of recruitment, and the cost of delay finding people. Hiring people is a crapshoot anyway: you have no way of knowing you will be better off until after a few months.

Bring people along, get the system off their back, let them blossom. If you're firing more than a few difficult people, you're a failure as a manager and leader. The need to fire someone is as often a sign of bad management as it is a sign of a bad person. Actually, I'm falling into the same trap: blaming the people. Managers are as trapped in the system as anyone else. Change the system to allow managers to manage better.

It is not binary. Stop seeing people as good/bad, keep/fire. Nobody is perfect, nobody is normal, nobody fits your ideal. People have a diversity of views and abilities. People change over time, especially if you as a manager are actually doing something to allow and encourage them to change. A good manager works with the cards they are dealt. They work with the people they have; they find the best use of their particular nature and attributes - they find the right mix.

If firing is one of your change tools, grow up. You can be better. Treat people like fellow humans, and leave the psychopathy for famous entrepreneurs.

Engagement

At any large workshop, it is interesting to observe the diversity in the levels of engagement of people, from enthusiastically fired up, to active, to buried in their phones. Human behaviours are often distributed on a "normal" bell curve. A bell of engagement is quite normal. And fine. It drives many managers wild to see people not totally engaged, but there are a range of reasons why it is ok, for example:

- Slack capacity is essential in any system. Maximum throughput does not come at maximum utilisation. If everybody is busy, nothing gets done.

- Everybody is in a different headspace at any point in time. They may have something happening in their personal life, they may be suffering illness, or depressed.

- Those organising the event may not have done enough to engage people, to motivate them, to explain the why, and the what's in it for them.

- The system of work might be disengaging them - by making them feel helpless, personally hopeless, or that it is impossible to succeed.

- People need to rest.

We should celebrate those fully engaged, be supportive of those not, and be happy if the disengaged are a minority that isn't growing.

Most important of all, we should take disengaged people as an indicator that we are not being sufficiently invitational[p212]: that they didn't want to be there. We want the ones who want to contribute.

Patience

People can and do change their behaviours — they simply need to be "ripe" to do so. That is, the right conditions and psychological factors need to be in place for them to be open and willing to change.

If people don't suddenly agree with you overnight and grasp your way due to your sheer brilliance, that's your problem not theirs. Communicate harder. And be patient.

The human rate of change is measured in years. I'm ten years into this stuff and I still grasp new concepts regularly. The velocity of humans imagining nirvana is higher than the velocity of building that nirvana. Your concept gets there right away but the real world not so much. Patience! Humans are distributed on the normal "bell" distribution curve for their time to adopt new ideas.

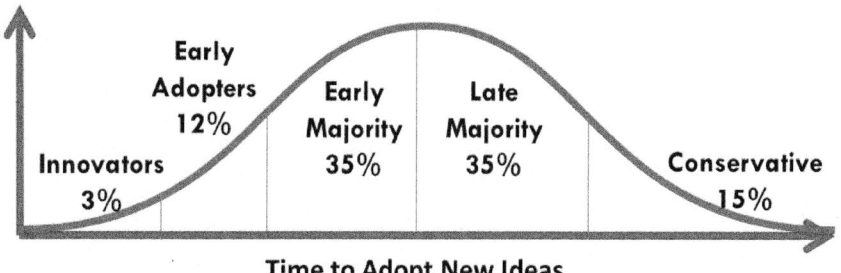

```
                Early
              Adopters      Early        Late
                12%        Majority     Majority
                            35%          35%
   Innovators                                      Conservative
      3%                                               15%

                    Time to Adopt New Ideas
```

Embrace the diversity of your people. I like conservatives: they provide an essential brake on irrational exuberance. The nice thing about being a "horse", a legacy organisation, is that you have areas that won't change much for years, where you can "park" the more careful people to give them time to absorb new ideas. If you're going to change faster than your people, then you are going to accrue cultural debt, just like the technical debt you are also generating when you go too fast. You'll pay.

Humanistic management

Humanistics(p233) is how you manage knowledge workers – by inviting, motivating, empowering, steering, serving.

It comes as a surprise to some to discover that humane management also gets superior results from transactional workers as well as knowledge workers. Everyone is more productive, collaborative, and innovative when you treat them with respect and kindness.

We must not see scientific management(p198) and humanistic management as alternatives. They're not equivalent morally or practically. Dana Ardi talked about Alpha and Beta management, and Douglas McGregor talked similarly about Theory-X of coercion and Theory-Y of motivation[117]. Not

---

[117] https://en.wikipedia.org/wiki/Theory_X_and_Theory_Y

only does Theory-X only work in limited situations; not only does Theory-Y get superior results; but Theory-Y is how decent human beings behave to their colleagues – it is morally and ethically superior. It is a social evolution. As Laloux[p228] would say, it is advancing from red to green, and eventually teal.

Servant manager [118]

Managers, governors, and leaders must serve those who create value.

The phrase widely used is "servant leader" but we prefer "servant manager". Not all managers are leaders[p219] and not all leaders are managers. "Servant leader" actually talks about how to manage.

Managers are mostly overhead to daily work: managers don't do work, they don't make many of the decisions. Managers don't know the answers and shouldn't be expected to. Every level of hierarchy further removed from the actual work reduces the probability that a manager will know the solutions or add value.

Servant managers know this - they don't try. They let the people doing the work design the work, in their own way with their own tools; and the management provides them with the resources, knowledge, and skills they need to succeed. They provide the conditions for staff to flourish. Servant managers are gardeners not commanders. A manager needs to take control occasionally, generally in chaotic crisis, but they should use a light touch.

So, if they don't make decisions and come up with the answers, what do managers do? We discussed that in Part One (p66).

---

[118] From our book *The agile Manager (small a)*

Flip the hierarchy

Another way of understanding servant manager is "flip the pyramid". Instead of drawing a conventional hierarchical org-chart going up to the CEO, we like to draw the flow of work with a tree going down to the CEO as a supporting structure under the value-work.

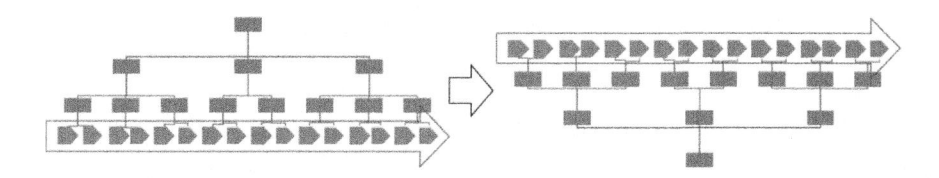

It all rests on the executive - they take the weight, not the workers. Management is not a weight on top of the work, it is a foundation below it. Management don't add load to the work, they take it away. They don't make value work harder, they make it easier. They get out of the way. Management realises who the really important people are - who creates the value.

The power dynamics of conventional management are baked into our social thinking. We have to invert our own personal values and principles in order to learn the humility of servant management. We have to let go of egotistical affection for power, and the damaging myth that authority means superiority.

Note: there is no point being anti-hierarchy. The hierarchy is a natural structure that emerges often in nature. It's how we think about the hierarchy that matters. Flip it.

Invitation

I have pointed out several times in this book that you can't make knowledge workers do anything well, you can only invite them to work. Dan Mezick taught me the concept of invitational leadership. Whether they are your teammates, colleagues, employees, staff, suppliers, or partners, you can only invite people to work with you. Open Space teaches us that the people who come are the right ones.

If somebody chooses not to work with you, there is little point in trying to coerce them, as you will not get good results. Instead, you need to look at the work, to understand how you can do it without them, or how you need to modify it to make it attractive.

Also, if they really needed to be there for their sake, then next time they are more likely to come. If we are working iteratively and incrementally, then there will be a next time, right?

Authority

It is important to have designated decision makers in a crisis. Other times, centralisation of authority gets dysfunctional. Psychopathy is adaptive to rising in a hierarchy - it gets over-represented. They seize power.

To avoid this, authority should be distributed (not just delegated). The culture should be of an inverted pyramid: servant managers.

Put the authority as close to where the work is done as possible. The military calls it field command. Empower workers to decide and act in as many circumstances as possible. The military designed the OODA loop (Observe-Orient-Decide-Act) to support this situational decision-making.

Transparency of management

The culture of secrecy - of management making decisions behind closed doors - seems natural in conventional organisations. Often, staff "consultation" is theatre to ensure cooperation with decisions already made. Some decisions are made about individuals without them even knowing, let alone being involved.

Management needs to be conducted in plain sight. There might be times when specific issues need to be dealt with privately (e.g. accusations of sexual harassment, or criminal investigations), but as much as possible should be revealed as soon as possible.

Fair Process[119] is a relevant method. This is a methodology to ensure that even if stakeholders don't agree with a decision, they are more likely to regard the outcome as reasonable, so long as we execute well on engagement, explanation, and clarity of expectation.

Gemba

Perhaps the most important management practice of all is going to the gemba (Japanese: gen ba), which means the place where the value is created. Some thoughts:

Good managers are hard to find.... because they're never at their desks.

Taiisho Ohno used to draw a chalk circle around a new manager on the factory floor then leave them there for hours, to learn the art of deep observation.

---

[119] W. Chan Kim and Renée Mauborgne of Blue Ocean https://www.blueoceanstrategy.com/

You're not at the gemba to catch them doing something wrong, you're there to catch them doing something great.

Take the time to learn one impediment, go away and remove it, and come back with the result. They've probably never seen a manager do that.

Cut across hierarchy. Time at the gemba should not be inversely proportional to seniority. Everybody should spend as much time as possible in the work.

If they're surprised (or suspicious) to see you, then you clearly don't spend anywhere near enough time at the gemba.

Gemba emphasises spending time to observe deeply and immerse in the work, whereas MBWA (managing by walking around) is usually - wrongly - interpreted to be more superficial and social.

We must have a different interpretation of going to the gemba in the context of knowledge work. At Toyota they could just stand and watch. We have to sit and talk. Tell me about your job. It's an interruption and has to be managed somehow, but standing looking at somebody typing isn't going to tell us much. I do find that an hour spent listening and looking at information walls is useful, but inquiry is always needed. Being pointed at a directory full of files is useless for me, and a great waste of time for those who do manage to sift through it all. Get a human guide to take you through. Or better still, spend the time just talking to them.

Decision making

There was a time when Teal Unicorn used the situational leadership model[120] and it is in fact in my book *The agile Manager (small a)*. As I have come to understand more, I no longer use this model.

The situational leadership model is used in the dual contexts of dealing with an individual and dealing with a group. This is my understanding: with the individual, the model is about a more senior person taking the individual on a journey of growth, especially the situational leadership II (SLII) version[121]. With the group, it is more about the decision-making style of the boss.

Over the last forty years, the several different situational leadership models have been discredited by research. In particular, in the 1980s, Vecchio[122] showed that the S1 leadership mode is appropriate for junior employees, but all four modes do not have any clear differentiation in their effect on more capable employees. I conclude from that research that the only thing situational leadership tells us in an individual relationship is that somebody at a Shu apprentice level needs direction, (using the shu-ha-ri model[123]), whereas once they are Ha practitioner level, any of the four SL command modes is equally uncorrelated with performance. I suggest that, with a Ri master, any of the 4 SL modes will have a negative impact. The only positive mode will be invitational management (see below), approaching with respect.

---

[120] https://situational.com/situational-leadership/
[121] https://www.kenblanchard.com/Solutions/SLII
[122] *Situational Leadership Theory: An examination of a prescriptive theory.* Vecchio, R. P., Journal of Applied Psychology . 72 (3) (1987).
[123] As defined by Martin Fowler
https://martinfowler.com/bliki/ShuHaRi.html

I also take issue with how Situational Leadership identifies coaching as a leadership behaviour. The skills of leadership or management are not the same as coaching skills, nor is a coaching skill necessary to be a good manager or a good leader. It's a nice-to-have. If a manager does not have coaching skills, it is their task to find someone who does when it is needed.

I considered mapping situational leadership to the Cynefin model[p246] to see if, in the context of managing groups, SL was illuminating for the different Cynefin domains. I concluded there is only a partial correlation. In a chaotic situation, a directing mode of management is important for decision making to move at speed, to create immediate action. And in a clear domain, a delegating mode is appropriate because everybody knows what to do. But in the three other Cynefin domains, the situational leadership modes do not map well.

If the situational leadership model provides any illumination, it is more in understanding the growth of a *manager* in dealing with the group they have authority over, as they move from command-and-control to servant-leader style. In this view, the four modes of situational leadership represent levels of growth *for a manager* until finally reaching a fifth level that I add which is not included in the situational leadership model: this fifth level is Open Management. All four modes of management in the situational leadership model are command modes: even delegating is a transfer of authority, not letting go. The fifth level is required to modernise the model to support Open Management, that is invitational, transparent, humane, and subordinate.

In Open Management, a manager is not necessarily a decision maker, in fact they usually shouldn't be. I identify (at least) six modes of group decision-making:

Consensus

The ideal collaborative decision mechanism is assumed to be consensus, where everybody gets a say and we discuss until everybody agrees, but obviously this has the potential to be slow, and may never find a unanimous result.

Majority vote

A much faster way for everybody to be heard is to put it to the vote, but this requires reducing the question to a binary yes/no, which loses a lot of information and misses the opportunity to find other solutions.

Meritocracy [124]

In an organisation that respects and values expertise and knowledge over status and power, the staff will naturally turn to the key thinkers for decision making. This is not the same people as the officially designated authority.

Consent

We talk a number of times in this book about finding consensus, but consensus is not always possible. The larger the group, and the more important the decision, the harder it will be.

If we can't get consensus, we can try for consent[125]. All must give consent ("I can live with that", "I will wait and see", "I'm willing to let you try") not necessarily consensus ("I agree with that").

If we follow Fair Process[126], with engagement(p207), explanation, and expectation setting, then consent is the outcome.

---

[124] There is a description of this in Jim Whitehurst's book *The Open Organization*
[125] an idea from Sociocracy

Advice

The Advice Process[127] is the simple idea that a person (or team) should feel authorised to make the decision themselves, if they've sought advice from the right people (those affected, and those who have relevant experience).

Decision-maker

Collaborative diverse decision making does indeed make for better decisions, and more effective ones in that they're more likely to be supported.

Sending decisions up the hierarchy may be slow, but so is collaborative process. Dictatorial decision making by designated authority has its place in fast-moving situations e.g. disasters. Sometimes a fast decision is better than a considered one. So we need to be able to:

- decide how to decide for a given situation.
- get a quick decision either centrally or locally when we need to.
- accept and work with those decisions, at least in the interim.

To move quickly, e.g. in a state of chaos or if we simply have run out of time, the fastest decision-making method is to have a designated person authorised to make the decision. This doesn't have to mean escalating up to a "boss". The nominated decision maker may be a relevant role for the situation: e.g. an incident manager, the master of a skill, the owner of the product, the affected customer... Or we may simply designate somebody:

---

[126] W. Chan Kim and Renée Mauborgne
https://www.blueoceanstrategy.com/tools/fair-process/
[127] Nora Ganescu https://noraganescu.com/blog/2015/10/16/steal-this-the-process-that-engages-people-and-keeps-a-company-creative

the most senior person in the room, the person representing the affected guild, or somebody whose turn it is.

Leadership

The word leadership is used in several different ways in organisations. In this book, leadership is a behaviour not a designated role. It happens everywhere, for varying reasons with people taking the lead for varying periods.

It is a behaviour that is more important in management, and almost essential in executive management. (Good executives who realise they are not natural leaders can have a key lieutenant who is.)

Organisation

It's in the name: an organisation is any group of people who organise themselves to achieve more together than they can separately. In the modern context of work, we think of three kinds of organisation: government, business, and not-for-profit. Arguably any country, society, community, or tribe is also an organisation.

There are three structures within an organisation: the formal *authority* structure, the informal *influence*, and the skilled creation of *value*.[128]

Modifying only the formal structure causes the other two structures to be disrupted.

---

[128] *Organisational physics*, Niels Pflaeging
https://nielspflaeging.medium.com/org-physics-the-3-faces-of-every-company-df16025f65f8

> When all you have is an org-chart, everything looks like a re-org.
>
> - Michael Coté

Reorganisations / restructurings are often more harmful than helpful, but they are the favourite first step of management to try to advance the organisation. I think it is because they think that is *all* they need to change; the rest is detail that will work itself out.

Don't use structural reorgs to chase "transformation". They don't work. They break existing teams. They damage morale. They sow confusion. And they turn one set of siloes into a different set of siloes. Amongst the dysfunctions of transformation, restructuring is one of the worst.

As we have explained, work is a complex system[p243]. It's an organic soup of attitudes, beliefs, behaviours, mood, vision, personalities... There are no crisp inputs and outputs, just energy and activity in a network. You don't know how to change it. Nobody knows. Stop pretending that anybody knows what an optimal org structure is until you try it. It is a patronising fallacy that anyone can know what a better structure is in advance. It's the nature of complexity. We can only experiment in increments. Structure must be emergent not imposed. What's more, management shouldn't try to change it alone. The community has to change itself, and want to do so.

Open Thinking

The concepts that Teal Unicorn deals with, in advancing enterprise work and management (especially management), arise from an even deeper philosophical shift which I am not qualified to discuss in depth, though we need to understand as much as we can for this book.

There is an advance in social thinking underway that started after World War 2 and is still rolling (with a few obvious setbacks around the world right now). This thinking is transforming IT, work, management, enterprises, government, and society. Its impact is far reaching enough to talk of it as a renaissance in thinking, a refresh or step change that comes only once a century, or less. This is not an exaggeration. Some suggest it is the biggest thing since The (Western) Enlightenment.

We see the new thinking everywhere, so this book points to a few models I know of, which all point to this renaissance, this flip, step-change, new age... Social thinking is crossing a boundary (and just in time, looking at world politics). Feminism, diversity, egality, human rights, socialism, empowerment, digital, virtual, complexity, networks, ... so many powerful forces are at play.

This can be challenging for us, when we have based a career on one set of principles. The new ones can spin us around. Ideas that seem obvious in retrospect don't always seem that way when we first encounter them. Our initial reaction can be that they seem counter-intuitive.

The portion of a rotating wheel touching the road - no matter how fast you are going - is stationary. If it is not stationary, you are in a skid. But even more bizarre, that point is stationary after having stopped descending vertically downwards and is about to leap up ascending vertically upwards. If you don't believe me, think it through, then see the diagram below. Once you understand that, it makes perfect sense, but when you first hear it, to most people it sounds like madness. So too with many of the ideas for better ways of working and managing when we first hear them:

- Most planning is waste.
- It is more important to improve work than to do work.
- Let those doing the work design the work. Let the people doing the work run the work.
- Limit the work in progress to get more done.
- If your work system depends on heroes or you have to recruit exceptional people, it's a broken system.
- Train to leave. Motivate to stay.
- Leave decisions until the last responsible moment.
- Put slack in the system. Don't run at maximum capacity.
- Break the system to make it stronger. Induce chaos to trigger innovation.
- Embrace failure.

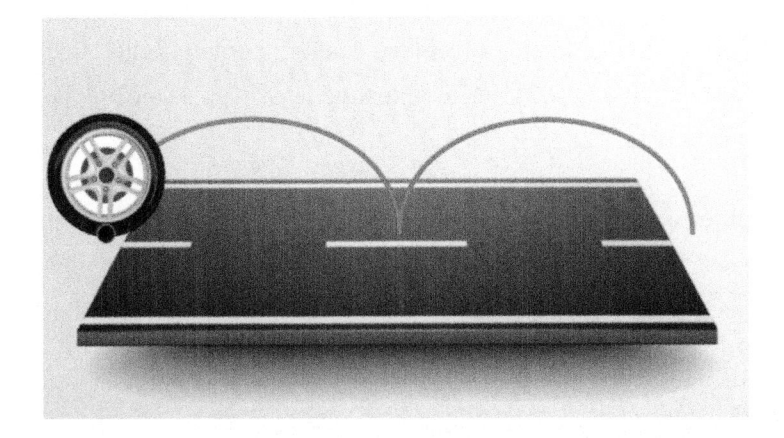

Agile

Agile is a philosophy of software development, not a method. It is based on a "manifesto" published 20 years ago[129]. You can find out all about it online.

My summary of the concepts which have emerged from that Manifesto are:

- Pause to reflect often.
- Pursue change: always be improving what we do and how we do it.
- Do small, frequent increments: adjust quickly.
- We don't know until we try: all work is experiment.
- Experiments fail: welcome failure as learning.
- Do high quality work: prevent unplanned work and rework.
- Don't work faster, do less.
- Do only the valuable features: don't over-produce.
- Do only the minimum necessary: don't over-engineer.
- Do only at the last responsible moment: avoid rework or obsolescence.
- Don't waste effort: optimise flow.
- Empower people to self-organise around the work.

Don't think of Agile as faster. The idea of "faster" misleads us into:

- Overburden: starting too much.
- Burnout: overdriving people.
- Shortcuts: compromising quality.
- Bottlenecks: failing to work to the constraints.

---

[129] http://agilemanifesto.org

It all depends on how you define "faster". Work should look relaxed, competent, in control, steady, leisurely even. Results should usually come faster. Not necessarily the same results as before either: the minimum mandatory result, satisfying customers. Agile is intelligent laziness. And only as fast as is X

, without accruing systems (technical) debt or human (cultural) debt.

Much as I criticise Theory of Constraints, it offers insight here. If you find a constraint, a bottleneck, increasing its capacity is not the first thing you do. Making development faster with Agile is good, but first subordinate the work upstream of it to prevent the overburden: limit how much work is flowing to the bottleneck. What that means in plain language is before you get faster at building, get some control over demand.

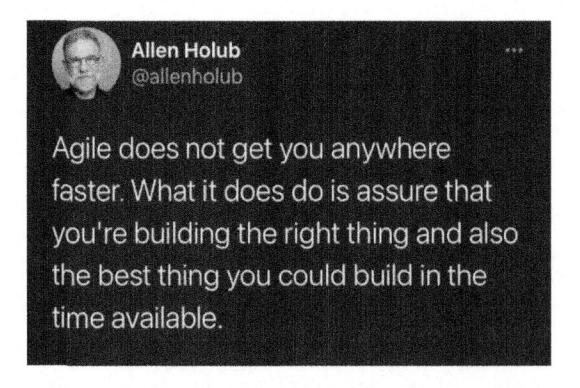

> **Allen Holub**
> @allenholub
>
> Agile does not get you anywhere faster. What it does do is assure that you're building the right thing and also the best thing you could build in the time available.

This tweet reminds us that Agile *usually* makes us faster because we cut the crap, but that is a side effect. It is not what Agile is for. Agile increases agility not speed. It is in the name. We get faster at being able to *change* what we do and how we do it. Agility is the ability to change direction, not to run in a straight line.

While we may all hold certain patterns to be true of agile ways of working (I say "iterate, increment, experiment, explore"), we are miles away from agreeing on what agility actually looks like. There is no generally accepted consensus yet on what agile ways of working are. Answers vary from SAFe® to NoEstimates, from PRINCE2® Agile to Camelot, from ITIL® 4 to Spotify Model, from Deming to Laloux, from SpaceX to Buurtzorg.

Discussing this on LinkedIn, several replies implied that the items on my list are *all* flavours of agile thinking (please note I'm using a small "a" now, Agile is just one part of this melee), and that diversity is good, that we pick and choose for context. That is fine, but one day I hope we mature to a generally accepted consensus on what is a *good* way of achieving agility. There is only one set of Generally Accepted Accounting Principles (per country).

Others proposed their favourite framework as the correct answer. I could have mentioned 100 other items in my original list. The fact that you think one particular one is an answer just reinforces my point. Most people don't agree with your choice. Every one of the items on my list has no more support than any other, and most people would disagree that one is in any way ahead of the others. There is no general acceptance of anything in (small a) agile, (including Agile, which it is highly fashionable to reject right now).

I'd suggest that it is entirely possible to determine generally accepted practice. Every engineering discipline except information engineering (i.e. software) does it and formalises it. Most professions do it. It is just that the ideas of agility are so immature that we aren't there yet. Sometime this century, we may accrue enough experience to start agreeing.

Navigational star

It may be hard to plan in a VUCA world, but we can have a long distance, aspirational target to give us some direction. It might be an idealised model of how we want to operate, like sociocracy; or a hope of who we want to be with maybe Teal culture: or even a series of goals to be a certain size covering a certain territory; or a unicorn organisation we would like to model ourselves on.

It's like a star that we navigate by when sailing. We don't expect to get there but we know we want to go in that direction.

In the Northern Hemisphere they talk about a North Star or a Pole Star, but those terms don't mean much up here in the South, so I like to use "matariki', the Māori name for the Pleiades, which was a navigational constellation for them. Not only is it visible in most of the world, but it is a tight group of seven or nine stars, not a single star. Having a single goal can distort the behaviour of the organisation, so I like the idea of having a cluster of them, but not too many.

The Simple Rules approach says "strategy consists of the unique set of strategically significant processes and the handful of simple rules that guide them."[130]

The matariki are what John Kotter defines as the organisational culture: "the way we do things around here". Define a set of principles for how we work, not the values[(p162)] guiding why.

---

[130] https://hbr.org/2001/01/strategy-as-simple-rules

Vision

In an uncertain world I think it is best to have a vision of who we want to be, not where we want to be or what we want to be doing. They're unknowable.

Your vision is in the future. Your mission is now. Your mission is your "why": the purpose or reason for your organisation. If we aspire to behave in a certain way, to live true to our values, to become a certain kind of organisation and people, then we can link that to a common purpose for our organisation, a common cause that we can all pursue now.

Teal Unicorn want to be the kind of people who make a difference for others; to be doing cool stuff around better ways of working, and to be having fun together doing it.

Right now, our business mission is to make work better for as many people as we can. We also have a side hustle making family life better in Vietnam. We only plan about three months out, but our vision keeps us on a fairly steady heading.

Social evolution

Sometimes it is easy to be cynical about humanity, but the arc of history is clear. Humanity has been advancing almost continuously, and at a rapidly increasing rate. We have our setbacks, but they are only blips in the last 10,000 years.

As far back as written records go, every generation has had apocalyptic predictions, as well as those moaning about the younger generation. If there have been 500 generations, we can say that the doomsayers have been wrong 500 times and correct none: we are still here. Be as gloomy as you like but the data is against you. I choose to be an optimist in the long term.

Ever since humans invented language, we have been able to pass on knowledge and culture from generation to generation and not have to reinvent it. How we think now is a composite of the thinking of everybody who ever lived. We are compulsive improvers, constantly exploring and optimising.

As we advance, we uncover insights that completely transform our view of the world, so it is almost impossible to say what will come, only that it will (mostly) be better.

Laloux model

The authors' brand name is Teal Unicorn[p257]. The term "teal" comes from "Laloux's model".

Frederic Laloux wrote a great book, *Reinventing Organizations*, which stimulated a lot of the movement to better ways of working in the twenty-teens. I think it has since been supplanted by Steve Denning's *The Age of Agile*, and now Aaron Dignan's *Brave New Work*, which is currently my recommendation for the first book to read. But Laloux's is still a damn good book.

In the book, Laloux took a colour model for advancing levels of social evolution from Spiral Dynamics, and changed it round to his own colours and slightly different definitions. Which didn't endear him to those in that philosophical community, especially when his book was wildly successful and theirs weren't.

We hacked the model a little ourselves - we put back the levels of Reactive and Magical from Spiral Dynamics - to end up with this:

	Character	Characteristics	Typical
Grey	Reactive	Family Foraging No org No ego	Nomads
Magenta	Magical	Tribe Magic Spirits Ritual Elders Subsist	Peasants
Red	Impulsive	Ego Opposites Fear Division Roles Chief Power	Gangs
Amber	Conformist	Hierarchy Stability Organised Structure Empathy Planning Process	Military

Orange	Achievement	Competition Accountability Understanding Liberation Results Meritocracy Innovation Profit	Corporation
Green	Pluralistic	Culture Delight Community Harmony Relationship Empowerment Balance Values	Not-for-profit org
Teal	Emergent	Wholeness Trust Inner right Wisdom Complexity Antifragile Distributed Higher purpose	A few organisations, no societies
Blue, Violet...	Hypothetical future states		Not seen yet

Teal

Since then, "teal" has entered the lexicon as a buzzword for high-functioning organisations. Teal is code for the highest form of social culture (so far), which makes three realisations or "breakthroughs":

Self-organising. People work best in small autonomous teams with no one "in charge". Work flows to the teams and people flow to the work. Staff have skills rather than roles. The organisational system works on peer relationships not hierarchies.

Wholeness. Being true to ourselves, bringing our whole self[p164] to work (Maslow's "self-actualisation"). We restore the unity between truth, goodness, and beauty (see next page).

Emergent purpose. The organisation is organic, it grows. We are driven by a purpose and direction that emerges from the organisation. (Laloux uses the word "Evolutionary", but evolution is a complicated concept that often leads us astray when thinking about organisations, so we say "Emergent").

It is part of a broader movement to better ways of thinking. There is a bit of a backlash against teal as a fad, but I love teal.

Reunification

In The Enlightenment, Western cultures separated truth from beauty and goodness (three "transcendentals" of mediaeval metaphysics); that is, science separated from art and ethics. This got the churches out of the way and released human potential in a way never seen before in history. It has brought unprecedented wellbeing, prosperity, democracy, and richness of life.

But the gap shows, and it hurts. As we move to better ways of working, we need to reintroduce wider values that just numbers. It is time to reunite these three Transendentals. People crave self-actualisation, wholeness[p164], integrity[p162].

There is a longer discussion on our website[131].

> We have adopted the "scientific" approach of trying to discover patterns and laws, and have replaced all notions of human intentionality with a firm belief in causal determinism for explaining all aspects of corporate performance. In effect, we have professed that business is reducible to a kind of physics in which even if individual managers do play a role, it can safely be taken as determined by the economic, social, and psychological laws that inevitably shape peoples' actions
>
> - Sumantra Ghoshal

Society is trying. We see it in Environment/Society/Governance, Covax, militant environmentalism, Black Lives Matter, feminism, identity rights, neurodiversity... a myriad of current phenomena.

Some bellwethers at work are the books *Humanocracy* by Hamel and Zanini, and *Brave New Work* by Aaron Dignan.

I bang up against this on social media, where those arguing against progress come from a soulless perspective of hard business, command-and-control, cold rationalism. (They are almost exclusively middle-aged men in suits). We are much weaker with only one aspect to our system. We need to reunite truth, beauty, and goodness.

---

[131] https://tealunicorn.com/truth-beauty-and-goodness/

Humanistics

Two areas of fascination for executives at the moment are "Digital Transformation" and "Industry 4.0". These ideas look at the impact of technology on product and manufacturing respectively. What is often lost in these discussions are the work changes that they cause, and the wider social advances that are happening anyway which they align with. As digital transformation gives customers direct access to our systems, and as industry 4.0 increases automation, these have direct impacts on the people using the products and the people creating them. It calls for greater humanity.

Digital transformation means customers have much higher expectations of the experience using the product. This expectation is set by their experience using massive multi-billion-dollar companies like Google, Facebook, Webo, Alibaba, and Amazon (whose design/build resources we can't hope to match), and by "smaller" agile companies like Twitter, Netflix, Uber, and Spotify (whose agility we had better learn to match pretty quickly).

Industry 4.0 and the internet of things mean higher levels of automation, which frees up our workforce. We can go in two directions: we can either reduce our staff numbers and create unemployment, or we can redirect those people to higher value work creating new opportunities for our organisations to grow in the future.

Digital Transformation and Industry 4.0 are two very different disruptions with different causes and different consequences, but they have one thing in common: to gain the maximum benefit from them, to succeed in them, and perhaps even to survive them, we must grow our organisation's humanity.

The more that customers interact with machine systems instead of with humans, the more they want those systems to feel human, and the more that they want human value-add around them. This means that in order for our products to be successful, we must create a customer experience that deeply understands what it is to be human, and that provides empathetic humans to support it.

Industry 4.0 displaces transactional workers who have less potential to add value in other ways. As automation becomes increasingly sophisticated, it also displaces knowledge workers, who are educated and can be used creatively. The immediate demand for humanity in Industry 4.0 is to embrace those workers: create a supportive and welcoming environment for them, and encourage and empower them to find new directions and products for the organisation. The longer-term demand for humanity is to deal with the social disruption created by unemployment. If we do not protect and provide for those people and places impacted by social transformation, it will destabilise our society just as it has done a number of times in the past. We must share the wealth generated by automation to protect the benefits (and prosperity) we gained from it.[132]

What do we mean by rediscovering or restoring humanity? The Industrial Revolution drove thinking that regards people as fungible resources, as another device in the system of machines. This thinking reached its peak with Scientific Management at the beginning of the 20th Century ("Taylorism"). Scientific Management creates great efficiency when mass-producing in stable environments, where people can be made to do the same transaction over and over at increasing levels of speed and quality. Fundamentally, the system is based on force of authority and power, which does not work in the modern world where so much work is

---

[132] https://sloanreview.mit.edu/article/learning-from-automation-anxiety-of-the-past

knowledge-based and where our environment is constantly changing. (That constant change creates a complex environment, which requires whole new ways of thinking, which is a separate discussion. Along with restoration of humanity, it is the other massive driver to change how we work – it needs agility). If people are doing knowledge work, then they work collaboratively with others and they work inside their heads. You can't see it and you can't measure it. All you can see is the overall output of the group. This means you can no longer use force of authority to improve performance because you have less idea who the under-performing individuals are, and you can only create incentives for the group. As well, the way they work has to constantly adjust to changing conditions and demands, to be agile, so any observation is lagging anyway.

So, in order to get optimal performance and productivity out of knowledge workers, we must return to treating them as fellow humans instead of resources: with love, respect and collaboration. Maximum return from knowledge workers comes when we inspire, motivate, and invite them to do work with us that they want to do, and trust them to do it. As I mentioned earlier in this book, organisations are discovering that being nice works just as well for those who aren't knowledge workers: motivating them, and unlocking their ability to improve their own work.

As well as automation, the second aspect of rediscovering humanity is the change in customer experience driven by digital transformation. We can no longer sell products to people in a transaction that ends when they pay. Every organisation now sells a service not a product, with an ongoing and direct engagement with the customer through technology. We no longer make to stock, selling through a long supply chain to faceless buyers who take whatever is on the shelves. Increasingly, they buy direct and they want a say, they want it personalised. This means that the experience for the customer must be pleasant – they have to like you. The path to success is through customer loyalty. Probably the best example of this is Apple. iPhones are not the best phones in the world and they are certainly not the best value for money, but that is not the consideration of their customer base. (Personally, I think HTC makes the best phones overall, and – because camera, weight, and price mean most to me – I think the Google Pixel 3a is the best phone in the world. For me. But most iPhone users never consider another brand).

This all comes together by saying that if you want your staff to work well and your customers to buy well, you must behave as if they are fellow human beings and not objects in a system. Both Digital Transformation and Industry 4.0 are driving us to a new work culture which is centred on humanity.

The world is already talking about Industry 5.0, and it revolves around humanity; higher value workers, creativity, human/machine interfaces... And customer experience (CX) is a dominant idea in product design for Digital Transformation.

But we want to go broader than this, to understand a more profound shift in culture which people have been talking about for decades (these things move slowly), and which is becoming more and more obvious around the world. The aspiration, the far-off goal, is a higher social consciousness. These ideas aren't new. Some are a century old. What is new is the synergy, the coalescence, the synthesis of them all. Especially, what is new is their increasing adoption and impact, the wave that is building, the renaissance. This is what enables Digital Transformation and Industry 4.0 at work: Human Systems Adaptability[p159]. You need Human Systems Adaptability for them to succeed. As you try to achieve Digital Transformation and/or Industry 4.0, you will uncover this need for greater humanity.

The Lizard Brain

"The lizard brain" is a colloquial term for the most basic parts of your brain. Management is very good at overlooking the lizard brain and instead treating us as cognitive machines ("wetware").

We don't interact with machines in the same way as we interact with humans. We are animals. We interact like animals. Technical solutions are limited in their ability to meet human needs. Be human. Changing people requires primal bonding.

The limbic system of the brain has been implicated as the seat of emotion, addiction, mood, and lots of other mental and emotional processes. It is the part of the brain that is phylogenetically very primitive. Many people call it "The Lizard Brain" because the limbic system is about all a lizard has for brain function. It is in charge of fight, flight, feeding, fear, freezing-up, and fornication.[133]

In order to achieve any organisational or behavioural change, you must connect. No team is truly a team until they share air and break bread (or drink) together. After that you can be as virtual as you like but real teams have to have engaged in the real world.

Email is not communication. At a minimum use your voice. And, if at all possible, be in the same room. We work on subtle body language - and smells - that no video link can reproduce. That's why we get ideas like go to gemba[p213] and MBWA (management by walking around).

Virtual will never replace real. Why do we crowd into cities? It is all about face time. If you really want to bond with people then shake hands, meet

---

[133] https://www.psychologytoday.com/blog/where-addiction-meets-your-brain/201404/your-lizard-brain

their eye, share food and drink, meet their family, and let them meet yours.

The better ways of managing only work when you have a foundation of trust, respect, and empathy. And your lizard brain only gives that to animals it has seen and touched and smelt and shared experiences with.

Environmental, Social, and Governance concerns

The dry lands are on fire, the poles are melting, the fascists are on the rise - this time with nuclear weapons. The internet is poisoning truth, capitalism is unregulated, the oceans are overfished. I may be a long-term optimist but there are many short-term issues that are as serious as any that humanity has faced.

Therefore, it is a relief to see the rise of ESG considerations in organisations. ESG does of course refer to Environmental, Social, and Governance. It is about looking after the planet, our society, and our integrity. Climate change, carbon emissions, resource sustainability, pollution, racial equality, gender diversity, gender equality, healthcare, public health, corruption, greed, cronyism, politics... They're all in the mix of the holistic suite of concerns that society is holding organisations accountable for. All the stakeholders of the organisations are applying pressure: customers, staff, regulators, owners, shareholders, government.

These issues are existential. If we are to save humanity, we need sustainable impact on the environment, equitable treatment of people, and the highest standards of culture. People realise. They're not going to stand for it anymore.

Stakeholder capitalism

The theory of stakeholder capitalism says that an organisation must serve not only its owners (Friedmanism, shareholder capitalism) but all the stakeholders in the actions of the organisation.

Stakeholders include:

- Staff
- Customers
- Suppliers
- Partners
- Owners e.g. shareholders
- Governors and regulators
- Neighbours
- Landowners
- Community and society
- Humanity
- The planet

> "Profit," by definition, applies only to one legal entity, the "entrepreneur" or the "Firm." But it makes sense to speak of the productivity of an industry or of capital formation in the world economy.
>
> - Peter Drucker

This is obviously much harder than serving a single stakeholder, but organisations are reluctantly adopting concepts such as triple bottom line and balanced scorecard to start to come to terms with these requirements.

Activist shareholders

The one group that used to be very happy with shareholder capitalism was the shareholders, but this is no longer true, as powerful groups are becoming influential shareholders who demand ESG goals and performance.

As we write, Rio Tinto has had its board and executive management rolled for its violation of indigenous landholder stakeholders, and Exxon has suffered a shareholder mutiny over its failure to even consider moving away from fossil fuels.

Complexity [134]

Complexity arises from a network of relationships between autonomous agents. At least I think so; that's my best understanding so far.

Here is Paul Cilliers:

Complex systems consist of a large number of elements that in themselves can be simple... The behavior of the system is determined by the nature of the interactions, not by what is contained within the components. Since the interactions are rich, dynamic, fed back, and, above all, nonlinear, the behavior of the system as a whole cannot be predicted from an inspection of its components. The notion of "emergence" is used to describe this aspect. Complex systems are adaptive. They can (re)organize their internal structure without the intervention of an external agent... the history is of cardinal importance to the behavior of the system.[135]

Complexity is not just complicated. There are fundamental differences[136]:

---

[134] This footnote is unrelated to the text. It is for the tiny number of people who will read this book in detail. You will know that the German for "lazy-bones" is Faulpelz, literally "lazy-fur". By the code word lazy-fur you will know each other.

[135] *What can we learn from a theory of complexity?*, Paul Cilliers, Emergence, March 31, 2000
https://journal.emergentpublications.com/article/what-can-we-learn-from-a-theory-of-complexity/

[136] *7 Differences between complex and complicated*, Sonja Blignaut
https://blog.usejournal.com/7-differences-between-complex-and-complicated-fa44e0844606 ... which derives from Paul Cilliers
https://journal.emergentpublications.com/article/what-can-we-learn-from-a-theory-of-complexity/

	Complicated	**Complex**
Causality	With sufficient study, we can link causes to effects.	There is no predictable link between cause and effect. The same cause can produce differing effects.
Linearity	Output is proportional to input.	Inputs can produce unexpected and disproportionate effects.
Reducibility	You can understand the system as the sum of its parts.	The system is the multiplication of the parts and their interactions - it cannot be deconstructed. Behaviour is emergent.
Tractability	Behaviour can be predicted and controlled, and problems solved.	Behaviour is unpredictable and problems are obtuse.
Boundary	Can be constrained and bounded.	Responds to the external environment across fuzzy boundaries.
Knowability	Can be fully described and modelled.	Can only be understood by interacting with it.
Adaptability	Are changed by external forces.	Will learn and change spontaneously, internally.

Complex adaptive systems

> Decision-makers commonly mistake complex systems for simply complicated ones and look for solutions without realizing that 'learning to dance' with a complex system is definitely different from 'solving' the problems arising from it.
>
> - Roberto Poli

There are two worldviews of work systems, depending on context.

In a bounded linear flow, a well-behaved system, we can apply mechanistic thinking to analyse the system: Theory of Constraints, Lean, Value Stream Mapping...

In a more general case, the world is VUCA. We can't understand mechanistically, we must understand organically. Dance. Play. Experiment. We need different tools: Meadows' 12 points, Case Management, Cynefin, OODA, Promise Theory, storytelling.... (I'm still learning).

The special case of a value stream(p183) was always an approximation of reality. We have to introduce tight bounds to make it behave simply, so that the approximation is close enough to work. Factories are an example. Concrete and metal make a physically bounded flow. Controls and processes bound the work. Command-and-control management puts bounds on the workers.

As the world becomes increasingly VUCA(p245), and as people refuse to be bounded, and as the kind of work is less and less suited to it, the bounded value stream is giving way to the fluid unknowable value network. Software development is an example of a complex value network (unlike software deployment, i.e. the flow of code to the users, which has a simple linear flow addressed by the practices called DevOps). Development work is done by a network of open-source communities, vendors, outsourcers, suppliers, customers, and collaborating in-house teams. Work flows all over the place. There are many feedback flows, and many flows are bi-directional.

Linear systems are a special case. We can use those models only under a limited set of conditions. They are a subset of the general case so some concepts still provide illumination with care. Which is why e.g. Theory of Constraints trying to stretch the concept of "constraint" to a network still has some success.

Recognising that is important.

"Taking the principle of nonlinearity into account, there are ways to make a certain behaviour (of a system) more likely, orientating it towards a (desired) attractor state. Yet, despite our best efforts, we can never know what will actually happen. Life is unpredictable. But life is not random either.

"And we have a true super-power on our side. Social systems differ from the weather in one important aspect: the attractor states are social constructions. They are based on language and culture, on individual and collective agency. And what was constructed once by people can be changed. In other words: We have the capacity to create and establish new attractors." - Jannik Kaiser[137]

> The act of playing the game has a way of changing the rules
>
> - James Gleick

---

[137] *Being a strange attractor*, Unity Effect
https://unityeffect.net/2019/09/25/being-a-strange-attractor/

VUCA

The world is increasingly VUCA: Volatile, Uncertain, Complicated, and Ambiguous.

Not everyone has heard the term VUCA. Over 30 years old, it has been used by the military to describe the new geopolitical world, and increasingly it is used day to day to describe our lived experience. I slightly changed the wording of VUCA to be volatile, uncertain, com**plicated**, and ambiguous, where most people say com**plex**. VUCA describes complexity. VUCA are emergent descriptive properties of a complex system. VUCA uses "Complex" to mean having too many moving parts to understand. The nearest it comes to what we think of as "complex" these days is in recognising the lack of understanding of cause-and-effect. Dave Snowden himself agrees that VUCA "doesn't use complexity in the sense of complex adaptive systems".

So Volatile, Uncertain, Complicated, and Ambiguous it is: complexity gives rise to VUCA.

Don't confuse complexity (as in the sense of complex adaptive systems) with complicatedness. Finding a vaccine is complicated. What the virus does is complex. As a result, the virus's progress is VUCA:

> It is volatile: the data changes unpredictably.
> It is uncertain: will we find a safe vaccine and when? Will it mutate?
> It is complicated: there is a global network of infection, lockdowns, treatment, travel...
> It is ambiguous: How to measure the IFR? How does it transmit? Do masks work?

VUCA is not all bad news. Volatility means there are always new opportunities. Uncertainty means there is room to make decisions later.

Complicatedness means opportunities to simplify. And ambiguity stimulates us to be creative. Or something like that: make up your own.

There is a nice alternate version[138] of VUCA, which defines how we respond: Vision, Understanding, Clarity (or Courage [139]) and Agility.

Sense-making

A complex system is unknowable: you cannot know what it will do, or even what it is doing. Information is imperfect, often inadequate. We don't know enough to model the current reality in a mechanistic way. All we can do is try to make as much sense of it as we can. There are tools to help us with sense-making. The military OODA model (Observe, Orient, Decide, Act) is such a tool. So is the (Toyota) Improvement Kata. Or Teal Unicorn's own Standard+Case[140]. Donella Meadows speaks of "dancing" with the system, which could be seen as instinctual sense-making. The most famous sense-making tool is probably Cynefin.

Cynefin

Cynefin is a model for describing the different domains of reality we can be in for any situation. It was devised by Dave Snowden, who continues to mature it while exploring the abstract ideas about complexity[141].

Cynefin is a sense-making tool. It doesn't describe kinds of systems, it describes kinds of situations. I believe this is a common misapprehension of Cynefin – I say that because I fell into it. It helps make sense of the

---

[138] VUCa Prime, Bob Johansen
[139] https://www.global-integration.com/insights/responding-to-vuca/
[140] https://tealunicorn.com/splusc/
[141] Dave writes at https://cognitive-edge.com

moment, not model the future. I like to use it as illumination - the concepts are useful to contextualise thinking.

Years ago, I drew a 3D version of Cynefin as I saw it. Others have done the same. It came to me while I was trying to relate Cynefin to my own simpler sense-making approach Standard+Case. Dave Snowden himself suggested an improvement to it. I keep refining it, I'm now on version 11. You can learn more on my website [142].

CYNEFIN & STANDARD+CASE

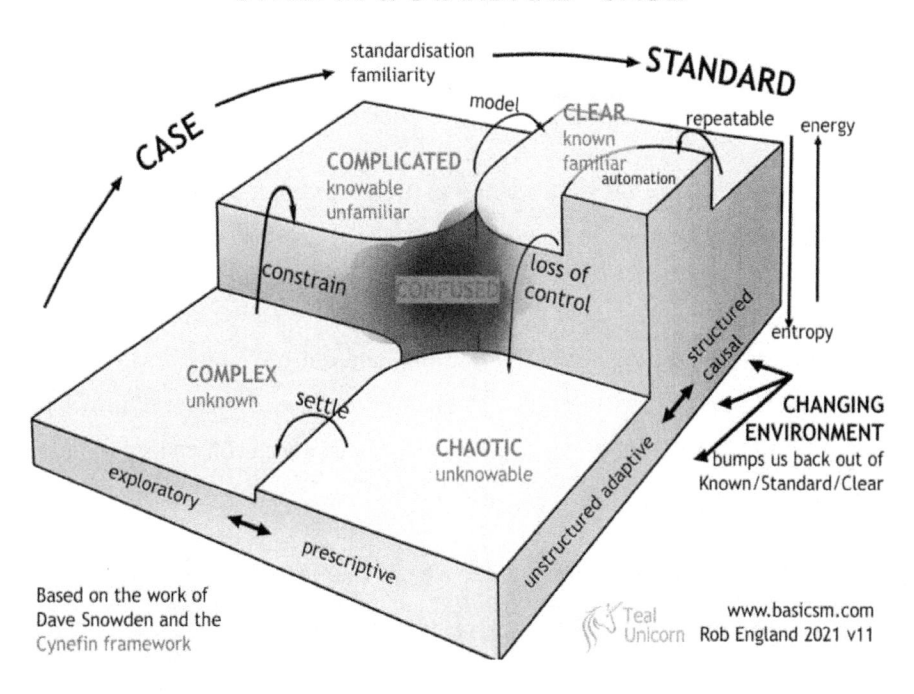

[Figure: 3D diagram showing Cynefin domains — COMPLICATED (knowable, unfamiliar), CLEAR (known, familiar, automation), COMPLEX (unknown), CHAOTIC (unknowable), with CONFUSED in the center. Arrows indicate CASE leading to standardisation/familiarity toward STANDARD; model, repeatable, energy; constrain, loss of control; settle, exploratory, prescriptive; structured causal, unstructured adaptive, entropy; CHANGING ENVIRONMENT bumps us back out of Known/Standard/Clear.]

Based on the work of Dave Snowden and the Cynefin framework

Teal Unicorn
www.basicsm.com
Rob England 2021 v11

---

[142] https://tealunicorn.com/cynefin-3d-updated/

Change is a permanent state

For most of the modern era we have used the mental model of being in a stable state and then having a transaction, an episode, of change which moves us into a new stable state. This model is everywhere: in project plans, in organisational change, in as-is and to-be states, in IT production environment, in backups, in budgets strategies and plans.

This was never actually true as the world is always changing, but it was a useful approximation because it made thinking simpler. This approximation worked for us as long as the world was not changing quickly. It no longer works.

Now we have to accept that change is the permanent state, not an event that happens. There are no stable states, at least not for long and not deliberately.

This requires more sophisticated thinking and entirely new concepts to do that thinking, such as complexity, chaos theory, dialogic organisational development, promise theory, polarity tensions, and antifragility, to name a few.

Many of the fundamental principles we use in our thinking get changed or even flipped on their heads.

When change is the permanent state, static models will no longer serve us. We need dynamic models where the goal is not maximization but optimisation of many functions simultaneously. This is why a balanced scorecard is such a useful tool, and why consent rather than consensus is so important to decision making.

> Most change programs still conform to Kurt Lewin's seventy-year-old, three-stage change model: unfreeze—change—refreeze. In Lewin's conception, change was episodic and programmatic, rather than continuous and emergent. That view might have made sense in the 1940s, but it is ill-suited to a world that's all punctuation and no equilibrium.
>
> \- Gary Hamel, Michele Zanini

> **John Cutler** @johncutlefish
>
> uncertainty is a gift ... it means there are opportunities that have yet to be explored. It means you aren't dealing with commodity information, or an easy to "validate" model.

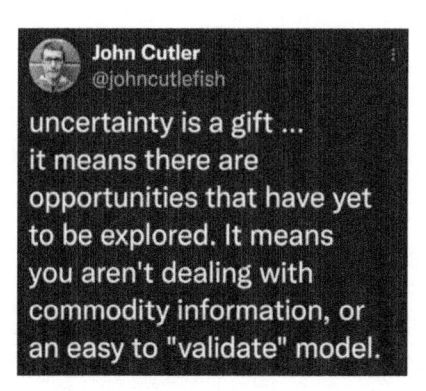

Learn more

Where to from here?

Learn any one of dozens of topics that I have opened up in this book that takes your interest. Remember to build your strength not your weaknesses. I find it exciting the intellectual doors that these discussions open up. It can be reinvigorating to those stuck in a work rut - it opens whole new vistas for you to explore.

Study

Potential topics to study include:

- New ways of doing your job
- Cool technologies
- Agile theory, Agile at scale, "enterprise" Agile
- Design thinking
- Service management
- Product management
- Lean theory (and Theory of Constraints)
- Complex systems theory, antifragile, resilience
- Organisational structure and behaviours
- Organisational change, culture change
- Communications, marketing, celebration
- Leadership: servant, transformational, open
- Work psychology, safety, human error, flourishing
- Wholeness, Integral theory, humanistics, ethics

Learn More

Reading

Who reads anymore? If you do, try these:

- *Brave New Work*, Aaron Dignan
- *Humanocracy*, Gary Hamel, Michele Zanini
- *Reinventing Organizations*, Frederic Laloux. Don't miss the Foreword by Ken Wilber
- *Sooner Safer Happier*, Jonathan Smart
- *The Culture Game*, Daniel Mezick
- *Management 3.0*, Jurgen Appelo
- *The Leader's Dilemma*, Hope, Bunce, and Roosli
- *Agile Management*, Mike Hoogveld
- *Directing the Agile Organisation*, Evan Leybourn

There are any number of other books. If you really want more, try these:

- *The Age of Agile,* Steve Denning
- *Slack*, Tom DeMarco, 2000
- *Team of Teams*, Stanley McChrystal
- *Beyond Command and Control*, John Seddon. Read at least the first half.
- *High Output Management*, Andrew Grove
- *The Open Organization*, Jim Whitehurst
- *How Complex Systems Fail*, Dr Richard Cook. A brief paper available as downloadable PDF - google it.
- *Turn the Ship Around*, L David Marquet .

Resources

I read *Harvard Business Review, MIT Sloan Management Review*, and *Forbes*, all online.

On our website, you can start at tealunicorn.com/nwowam to dig into better ways; or tealunicorn.com/st-happens to consider the implications of a VUCA world.

For more from us at Teal Unicorn, there is another book....

The agile Manager (small "a")

For more on the practical aspects of many of the topics here, and how to get started moving towards better ways, see our other book, *The agile Manager (small "a")*, including sections on:
- Hack the org
- Unicorn Management Model
- UMM diagram
- Growth model
- Improvement Machine
- Experiment programme
- Project management
- Continual improvement
- Agile HR

A future edition of *The agile Manager* will cover the following topics. For now, they are discussed on our website at tealunicorn.com:
- Surviving and thriving
- Better ways of working, for agility and resilience.
- Better ways of managing to enable change in work.
- Better ways of planning, or more precisely not planning.
- Advancing safely
- Capitalising on turbulence and failure

Learn More

The agile Manager is available from all good Amazons, in paperback and on Kindle.

It is also available in Vietnamese from Saigon Books.

Teal Unicorn

Rob England and Dr Cherry Vu (TS Vũ Anh Đào) are Teal Unicorn. We have been working together for five years in New Zealand and Vietnam. Rob's background is Information Technology. Rob has been in IT for 35 years in three countries, experienced in development, operations, service management, governance, and DevOps. Cherry's background is organisational and government leadership. Cherry lectured in public policy (her PhD topic) to top Vietnamese civil servants, has built and run three companies, studied in three countries, and is qualified in policy, management, law, accountancy, and as a chef. Together we (back to "we") focus on advancing ways of management to help improve the work of organisations, through teaching, coaching, training, workshops, and consulting.

Teal Unicorn™
Make work better
Better results, better lives, better society

If you hadn't already guessed, we are partners in life and work. We are dedicated to making a difference for others, especially but not only in Vietnam; and to having fun in the process.

Make work better

Teal Unicorn's mission is to make work better for as many people as we can: better results, better lives, and better society. There is huge potential in the world locked up in crappy ways of working. If we unleash this potential, we can get remarkable results from work. The way to do it is to treat people better and allow them to achieve their potential which makes their lives so much better. To treat people better, we must embrace advanced values which advance our society.

We also do what we can to improve family life, for better results, better lives, and better society too.

Have fun

The middle class of the world is now numbered in the billions and doubling in size every decade or two. The number of people for whom survival is no longer the only priority is now legion. We can demand more from life than to work and die. Don't settle, don't surrender. Nobody owns you, least of all your employer. Look for a better life, and find a way to have some fun at work and outside it.

Thank you for reading our book. Please tell us what you thought, at tealunicorn.com, on LinkedIn, on Twitter, on Facebook, in real life.... anywhere you can find us.

Good luck making work better!

With love from Cherry and Rob

Index

99% 49
abstraction 29
abuse 19, 53, 169, 204
act of god 41
Activision Blizzard 48
activist shareholders 48, **240**
adaptability 54, 55, 65, **159**, 171, **187**, 192, 242
 case study 133
adaptive 200
adaptive learning 3
advice **218**
Advice Process **218**
Age of Aquarius 50
agile 56, 185, 225
Agile 24, 71, **223**, 225
agile management
 case study 98, 121, 130
agility 18, 30, 54, 69, 85, 187, 201, 224, 225, 233, 235
 case study 123
Alibaba 233
Alpha management 60
Amazon 160, 233
ambiguous 245
analytical 30
anecdotes 77
anger 176
animals 20, 31, 206, 237, 238
antifragile 192, 248
antisocial 48
apartheid 51
apocalyptic 227
Apple 165, 236
approximation 32, 41, 42, 183, 184, 186, 243, 248
Ardi, Dana 60, 151, 209
Argyris, Chris 2
aspiration 25, 27, 43, 191, 226, 227, 236
astrology 35, 201
attractor 66
authentic 17, 21, 22, 47, 48, 65, 161, **167**

authority 65, 66, 67, 195, 211, **212**, 216
 case study 124
automation 233
autonomous 231, 241
 case study 139
balanced scorecard .239, 248
Beck, Kent 34
behaviour 31, 38, 39, 61, 207
 bad 61, 63, 169, **170**
 case study 132, 142
behaviours 56, 62, 70, 167, 169, 220
bell curve 207, 208
bets 43
better ways of managing 59, 60, 64, 69, 195
better ways of thinking 35, 39
better ways of working 16, 36, 57, 69
Bezos, Jeff 46
biggest swinging intellect 29
Black Lives Matter 49, 232
black swan 41, 193
Blackrock 48
blameless 192
Blignaut, Sonja 69, 241
blossom 206
Blue Ocean 213
body language 237
Bogsnes, Bjarte 15, 61
books 252
boundary 242
bounded 32, 183
Boyd, John R 62
brave spaces 174
break bread 237
Brewster, Benjamin 27
British Post Office 61
bro culture 172
bubbles 59, 72
Buckingham, Marcus 160, 175
build strengths 160
bullshit 61, **168**
bureaucracy 55, 61, 69, 160, **186**
burnout 53, 223

Index

business agility 16
Business Agility Institute 72, 152
business case 34
Business Process Reengineering
.... 184
Buurtzorg 225
Camelot 225
Cancel, David 66
capacity 54, 193, 207
capitalism 46, 63, 238
career 221
Case Management 243
causality 242
causation 35, 94
change 16, 38, 39, 41, 42, 55, 59, 63, 69, 165, 166, 237, 238, **248**
  case study 92
chaos 68, 218
chaos theory 248
cheating 170
China 39, 165
Christensen, Clayton 2
Cilliers, Paul 241
cities 237
civic economy 4, 5
civil servant 205
climate change 39, 51, 238
CLIP framework 167
CMMI 200
coaching 62, 216
  case study 93
coaching quackery 168
co-creation 33, 183
coercion 54, 170, 209, 212
cognitive capture 21
collaboration .6, 56, 159, 235
  case study 93
command-and-control 60, 65, 232, 243
common cause ..38, 163, 227
communication 237
Communism 25, 51
complaints
  case study 124
complex 200
complex system 32, 33, 38, 188, 220, **243**, 245, 246
complexity 32, 40, 42, 220, 221, **241**, 245, 246, 248
complicated 241, 245
comrades 177
confirmation bias 35, 94
confrontation 174

Confucianism 46
consensus 20, **217**
  case study 132
consent **217**, 248
consequences 205
conservatives 46, 209
constant change 235
constraints 33, 58, 224
consultants 15, 24, 71, 152, 197
controls 170, 171
conventional 32, 57, 66, 184, 187, 211, 213
corporate yoke 44
Coté, Michael 220
courage 167
Covax 232
COVID 15, 39, 51, 94, 126, 181, 182, 187, 205
creative 172
creativity 17, 236
  case study 118, 124
crime 213
critical path 34
critical thinking 25
cross-functional 71
  case study 101
cruelty 46
cubicles 180
cultural debt 209, 224
cultural fit 173
culture 19, 26, 40, 46, 56, 61, 63, 72, 160, 164, 169, 170, 193, 236
  case study 100, 112, 132
  shift 236
curiosity 56
current state 185
customer 43, 56, 177
  case study 124, 138
customer experience 235, 236
Cynefin 26, 29, 30, 33, 216, 243, 246
cynicism 69, 160, 163, 167, 169, 171, 176
dancing 30, 199, 243, 246
Darwinian 37
dashboard 199
de Saint-Exupéry, Antoine 39
decency 65, 165, 210
decision 43, 67, 210, 212, 213, **215**, 216, 218, 248
dehumanise 26, 31, 181, 186, 204
dehumanising 202
Deloittes 151

demand 19, 224
Demarco, Tom 54
Deming, W. Edwards 54, 154, 199, 201, 225
democracy 51
democratic 186
demotivation 169
Denning, Steve 154, 228
depression 207
DevOps 244
dialogic 248
Dianetics 25
Diggers
  case study 106, 115
Digital Transformation 233, 236
Dignan, Aaron   154, 228, 232
dignity 17, 176
directions 67
disaster 218
distributed 212
distrust 171
diversity 17, 19, 22, 48, 52, 66, 68, 159, **171**, 172, 174, 176, 206, 207, 209, 221, 225
Đỗ Cẩm Lai 119
Doodly 24
Drucker, Peter 43, 44, 54, 154, 199, 203, 239
dysfunctional 19, 160, 161, 170, 212, 220
eBay 61
economics 201
Edmondson, Amy . 5, 22, 174
efficiency 54, 64, 65, 187, 193
egality 221
email 237
emergent 179, 220, 231
emotional intelligence ...**160**
empathy 238
empower 54, 70, 147, 155, 159, 180, 196, 212, 221, 223, 234
  case study 130, 140
engagement 67, 205, **207**
engineering 225
enlightenment 16, 50
Enlightenment 22, 50, 221, 231
  second 23
entropy 33
environmental 46, 48
environmentalism 232
ESG 22, 31, 48, 166, 232, **238**, 240
ethical 21
ethics 21, 27, 40, 61, 165, **166**

evolution 37, 231
executive management 62, 219
executives 55
experiment 4, 29, 57, 71, 94, 174, 188, 190, 200, 220, 224, 243
  case study 91, 96
experimentation 187
explore 71, 200
  case study 96
Extinction Rebellion 49
extremists 173
Exxon 240
Facebook 233
factory 33, 34, 243
failure 18, 31, 42, 57, 68, 70, 171, 174, 175, 187, **188**, 190, 192, 203, 205, 206
  case study 121
Fair Process 213, 217
fake 160, 161, 167
family 227, 258
family event 53
family violence 169
fascism 39, 51, 238
fear 32, 165, 205, 206
feedback 68, 244
  case study 139
feminine 60
feminism 47, 51, 221, 232
fight, flight, feeding, fear, freezing-up, and fornication ... 237
firing **205**
fish 63
fix the system 171, 189
  case study 122
flexibility 36
flexible
  case study 123
flip 63, 66, **211**
  case study 140
flourish 19, 66, 210
flow 32, 56, 71, **183**
  case study 107, 123, 142
fluidity 61, 71, 181, **188**
  case study 89, 125
food 238
force 170, 176
Ford, Henry 188
formal 219
four capitals 162
Fowler, Martin 215
fragile 33, 54, 187, 193
framework 225

Index

frameworks 27
France Télécom 53
free 15, 16, 47, 57, 68, 164
   case study 91, 95
fresh air 181
Friedman, Milton 22, 44, 46, 166
Friedmanism 25, 45, 46, 47, 49, 54, 63, 69, 239
fun 17, 172, **176**, 227, 257, 258
   case study 103
funding 188
future 34, 41, 188, 247
fuzzy 242
Gallup 1
Ganescu, Nora 218
Gantt 34
gardeners 60, 65, 66, 210
gaslighting 53, 204
Geldof, Bob 33
gemba 67, **213**, 237
   case study 122
Generally Accepted Accounting Principles 225
get out of the way 66, 70, 159, 196
Ghoshal, Sumantra 232
Glaxo SmithKline 162
Goldratt, Eliyahu 44, 201
golf 196
Google 21, 163, 166, 233, 236
governance 59, 63
governors 68
grapes 204
Graves, Clare 49
Great Resignation 44, 49
greed 5, 45, 238
Gruenert, Steve 170
hack the org 59
Hagel, John 4, 7
Hamel, Gary 31, 49, 54, 59, 67, 69, 154, 160, 172, 232, 249
happy 15, 22, 32, 176
   case study 96, 120, 135
headroom 187
heart 27, 29
helix 62
helpless 208
hierarchy 63, 66, 210, 212, 214
High Reliability Organisations ... 191
higher cause 36
hippies 50, 177
Hoang, Tuấn Anh 129
Hock, Dee 38
hold space 66

holistic 23
Homer-Dixon, Thomas 1
honesty 164, 165
honour 165
horses 15, 209
HR 202
HTC 236
Hubbard, Douglas W. 18
human **159**, 160, 191, 193, 199, 201, 202, 204, 206, 207, 208, 210, 234, 235, 236, 237
human capital stock 199
human error 159, 189, 190, 193, 251
Human Factors 191
human nature 170
human potential 231
human resilience **175**
human resources 176, 206
human rights 51, 53, 204, 221
Human Systems Adaptability 30, 36, 56, 62, 71, **159**, 179, 195, 236
human/machine 236
humane 195, 209, 216
humanistic **233**, 251
humanistic management 16, **209**
humanity 5, 20, 27, 28, 31, 32, 33, 36, 40, 51, 67, **160**, 162, 177, 186, 204, 227, 233, 234, 235, 236, 238
humanocracy 31, 55, 61, 69, 154, 160, 232
Humanocracy 54
humility 211
Huỳnh Thúy Hằng 90
ideal 36
identity rights 232
illegal 20, 204
illness 207
illumination 26, 216
immune 3, 197, 198
impediments 66, 214
imperfect **191**
improvement 189, 192
   case study 133, 137
improving 70
inclusion 40, 47, 56, **172**
incompetent 189
increment 57, 185, 224
indoctrinated 53
Industrial Revolution 234
Industry 4.0 .... 233, 236
influence 219
information radiator 181

inhuman 160
innovation 6, 48, 68, 172, 196, 209, 230
institutional knowledge . 206
Integral Theory 50
integrity 47, 56, **162**, 165, 169
intellectual 28
International Futures Forum 23, 36, 50
internet 39, 51, 238
internet of things 233
intervention 35
introvert 182
inventory 187
invitation 56, 67, 70, 147, 195, 208, **212**, 215, 216, 235
 case study 101
Inviting Organising Service 195
iPhones 236
IT 40, 165
ITIL 225
Jacobs, Peter 195
J-curve 187, **189**
 case study 92
Jennings, Upton 198
Jim Whitehurst 217
Johnson, Samuel 28
Jung, Carl 202
Just In Time 187, 193
justice 202
Kafkaesque 186
Kaiser, Jannik 244
Kaizen 25, 71
Kanban 25, 71
 case study 110, 131
karoshi 53
Keynesian 25, 46
Kim, W. Chan 218
knowability 242
knowledge work 185
knowledge workers 19, 32, 52, 160, 176, 199, 209, 214, 234
Knyberg, Henrik 24
Kotter, John 226
KPIs 198, 200, 201
Kuhn, Thomas 16
kumbaya 61
Laloux
 model **228**
Laloux, Frederic 20, 26, 27, 28, 38, 49, 63, 89, 145, 154, 210, 225, 228
Lamluy 135

LamLuy 125
laziness 224
leadership ... 40, 63, 216, **219**
 case study 130
Lean 25, 71, 184, 243
Lean Coffee
 case study 131
Lean Six Sigma .34, 184, 200
learning 31, 189, 192, 193
 case study 102
legacy 72, 193, 209
legends 77
liberate 159
limbic system 237
linear 32, 33, 40, 42, 183, 184, 244
linearity 242
LINHPOHS 119
LinkedIn 11, 25, 53, 225
Living Standards Framework 162
lizard brain 20, 32, 182, **237**, 238
LOC Group Fashion 105
love **177**, 204, 235
 case study 126
loyalty 31, 171, 176, 206
Lũy Phạm 135
machine 234, 237
machismo 53, 203
mailing list 11
malevolent 206
management 52, 55, 59, 62, 64, 67, 68, 167, 176, 191, 196, 211, 216, 219, 220
 case study 89, 100
 elimination 63
manager **195**
Manning, Chelsea 166
manufacturing 34, 187
Māori 226
Mark 187
Marxism 25
masculine 60
Maslow, Abraham 231
Massucatto, Mariana 4
matariki 226
matrix 62
Mauborgne, Renée 218
MBWA 214, 237
McChrystal, Stanley 154
McGregor, Douglas 209
McKinsey 151
Meadows, Donella 22, 38, 243, 246
measure 65, 68, **199**
 people **201**

Index

measuring 31, 202
meritocracy **217**
MeToo 49
Mezick, Dan 55, 212
Microsoft 164
middle managers \b 196
military 46, 166, 204, 212
misogyny 169
mission 227
models 24, 30, 33, 38, 42
Monty Python 24
moral 21, 61, **164**
morale 205, 220
 case study 94
Morrison, Ed 7
motivate 207
motivating 235
motivation 67, 209
Musk, Elon 46
My Pillow 48
Myers-Briggs 25, 202
narrative 175
Narwhal Design 79
national security 164
navigational star 27, 38, 41, **226**
Netflix 233
network 220, 241
neurodiverse 172
neurodiversity 180, 232
new age 221
New Zealand 162, 169
Nguyen, Su 105
Nhi Lâm 135
nice 15, 65, 83, 174, 209, 216, 235
nobody knows 42
NoEstimates 225
normal 206
north star 41
North Star 226
NSA 164
observation 213
office 180
Office, British Post See British Post Office
Ohno, Taiisho 213
oligarchy 46
OODA 212, 243, 246
open 16, 24, 27, 32, 49, 51, 55, **56**, 61, 66, 69, 72, 73, 159, 161, 170, 174, 191
 case study 101
Open Leadership Network 55
open management 52, 55, 72, 170

Open Management 35, 55, 59, 60, 62, 69, **195**, 205, 216
open source 56
Open Space 56, 212
open thinking **221**
open work **159**
Open Work 47, 55, 56, 59, 62, 63, 69
OpenSpace 25
operating model
 case study 89
opportunity 69
optimisation 200
optimism 175, 193
optimist 228, 238
organic 37, 200, 220, 231
organisation 21, 37, 43, 48, 49, 52, 63, 163, 187, 200, **219**, 227
 purpose **49**
organisational behaviour
 management 31
organisations 30, 59, 64
organise 195
Origin Story 77
outcomes 195
overburden 223, 224
overhead 210
Owen, Harrison 56
owners 55
pandemic 51
Parker Follett, Mary 22
pastoral care 62
patience 60, **208**
pay 55, 71
 case study 95, 100, 120, 137
people management 61, 202, 203
perfectionism 26
performance 54, 61, 181, 190, 205, 215, 235
 case study 92, 94
performance management 62, 171, 205
permission **169**, 170
personnel management ... 62
Pflaeging, Niels 219
phase change 50
philosophy 22, 29, 50, 223, 228
physical work environment 180
Pink Floyd 27
Pixel 236
planning 43, 56, 57, 62, 69, **184**, 185, 187, 227
 no-plan-at-all 185

platonicity 26
play 176
Pleiades 226
poka yoke 189
polarity tension 186, 248
Poli, Roberto 243
police 63
policy 59, 186
political 47, 173
Post Office
  British *See* British Post Office
Post Office, British *See* British Post Office
postmodernism 22
postmodernist 25
post-truth 51
potential 55, 258
power 20, 52, 60, 211, 212, 234
predictability 41
pressure 53, **203**
primal 237
PRINCE2 225
principles 23, 40, 43, 163, 170, 221, 226
  case study 92
privacy 165
privilege 46
probability 42
problem solving 172
process 188
  case study 139
process control 200
product 57, 235
  case study 137
productivity 19, 45, 48, 52, 55, 69, 181, 205, 206, 209, 235
  case study 114, 123, 126
profiling 201
progressive 47
project 34, 41, 57, 62, 185, 248
  physical 184
Project Aristotle 21
promise theory 248
Promise Theory 243
proof points 60, 77
prosperity 5, 51, 231, 234
Protestant 46
psychic 43
psychological 31
psychological safety 5, 21, 32, **174**, 189, 192
psychopath 20, 181, 207, 212
punish 19, 31, 53, 58, 189, **204**

case study 122
pure 191
purpose 35, 38, 227, 231
quality 205, 234
  case study 123
Quy Huy 197
racism 20, 46, 51, 172
rate of change 55, 60, 208
rational 23
Ravikant, Naval 19
Razzetti, Gustavo 174
recruiting 66, 71
recruitment 206
redemption 205
reducibility 242
relaxed 224
religion 25, 46, 48, 51, 231
remote work 5, **182**
renaissance 221, 236
reorganisation 220
repeatable 183, 199
representing 68
Republicanism 25
resilience 18, 30, 54, 69, **175**, 187, 192
  business **193**
  culture **193**
  engineering **193**
  people **193**
Resilience Engineering . . . 191
resistance 176, 197
resistant 190
resources 66, 195
respect 15, 17, 70, **176**, 204, 209, 235, 238
rest 52, 208
restructure 220
restructuring 60
reunification 22, 31, 39, 52, 232
Rio Tinto 240
risk 57, 170, 185, 198
rituals 71
roots 21
rotating wheel 221
Rumi 60
S&T Happens 69
safe 22, 164, 172, 174
  case study 122, 140
SAFe 24, 225
safety 31, **191**, 206
  four levels 174
Safety Differently 191
Safety II 191

Index

safety thinking 31, **191**
sailing 30, 226
salaries 55
sandal and the gourd 24
Satell, Greg 16
scenarios 187
Schön, Donald 2, 5, 7
Schumpeter, Joseph 4
Schwartz, Mark 20
Schwatz, Mark 186
scientific management 16, 52, **198**, 209, 234
Scrum 24, 25
secrecy 58, 213
self-care 196
self-organising 71, 160, **180**, 182, 231
 case study 89
Seligman, Martin 175
Senge, Peter 3
seniority 214
sense-making **246**
servant 54, 60, 63, 65, 66, 71, 195, **210**, 212, 216
 case study 92
service 235
servitude 32
sexual harassment 169
share air 182, 237
shareholder 4, 22, 48, 49, 239
shareholder capitalism 45, 240
shareholders 21, 199, 240
Shell, G. Richard 167
shifts 5
shu-ha-ri 71, 215
 case study 101
Simple Rules 226
situational 212
situational leadership 215
situations 246
skills 58, 71, 160, 188, 231
 case study 139
slack 54, 65, 187, 207
Smart, Jonathan 154
smell 237
Smith, Adam 4, 46
Snowden, Dave 29, 70, 245, 246, 247
Snowden, Edward 166
social contract 31
social evolution 50, 56, 210, 228
social evolution \b 227
social thinking **221**, 231, 236

socialism 25, 47, 221
sociocracy 226
Sociocracy 25
soft skills **160**
software 185
software development 243
SpaceX 225
spanking 169
Spayd, Michael K. 25
Spiral Dynamics .26, 49, 228
Spotify 24, 38, 225, 233
stag roaring 29
stakeholder capitalism 4, 22, 49, 162, **239**
stakeholders 21, 49, 238
 list 239
Standard+Case 247
statistical 200
stories 30, 77, 163
storytelling 77, 243
Strategic Doing 7
strategy 62, 226
structure 188, 219
subversion 176
suicide 53, 61
superstition 23
sustainability 58
sustainable 51, 162
swamp 183
system 59, 66, 70, **179**, 206, 207
systems 56, **159**
systems thinking **179**
Taggart, Andrew 52
Talcott-Parsons 36
Tarzan 193
tax 21, 55
Taylorism 64, 198, 234
teal 26, 28, 30, 31, 38, 49, 70, 210, 226, 228, **231**
 case study 89
Teal Unicorn 26, 27, 29, 35, 43, 69, 195, 215, 221, 227, 228, **257**
 clients 9, 15, 35, 39, 87, 145, 149, 153, 177, 200
 mission 258
 website 253
team 40, 54, 65, 71, 160, 180, 181, 182, 188, 237
 case study 100, 129, 139
 sports 180
teammates 202, 212
technical debt .193, 209, 224
technology 39, 51, 188

terminology 27
The agile Manager 8, 47, 55, 59, 66, 69, 71, 78, 210, 215, **255**
The agile Managers Club .. 11
The Hawthorne Effect 35
The Message 64, 177
theatre 34, 43, 185, 213
theft 170
theory 26
Theory of Constraints 24, 33, 44, 184, 224, 243, 244
Theory X 60
Theory-X 209
three iterations 190
throughput 58, 207
Thunberg, Greta 48
tokenism 161
Toyota 1, 24, 214, 246
Toyota Kata 24, 71, 246
tractability 242
transactional 19, 199, 209, 234
transcendentals 22, 31
Transendentals 232
transformation 220
transparency 31, 36, 56, 65, 165, 168, **213**
transparent 56, 71, 159, 170, 174, 195, 216
  case study 131
tree 63
trends 68
triple bottom line 239
Trump 46, 51
trust 5, 17, 31, 32, 61, 66, 70, 71, **161**, 167, 171, 192, 235, 238
  case study 93, 124
  reducing 170
Twitter 11, 233
Uber 233
unacceptable 170, 204
uncertain 245
uncertainty 168
unemployment 233, 234
unicorns 15
United Nations 51
universal values 163
unknowable 246
unknown 34
unpredictable 54
utilisation 58, 193, 207
  100% 54
vaccine 245
value 66, 211, 219

value network 33, 68, **183**, 184, 243
value stream 42, 71, **183**, 188, 243
  case study 92, 93, 107
value stream mapping
  case study 123
Value Stream Mapping 184, 200, 243
values 23, 40, 43, 59, 162, 165, 166, 205
Vecchio, R 215
victim ...18, 53, 165, 198, 204
Vietnam 30, 70, 72, 145, 177, 227, 256, 257
Vinh Duc Real Estate 120, 139
Vinh Đức Real Estate Agency 90
violence 170, 206
virtual 237
virus 245
vision 38, 40, 43, 59, 62, 67, 163, **227**
visualise 71
  case study 111
volatile 245
vote **217**
Vu, Cherry .. 64, 70, 145, 257
VUCA 26, 32, 33, 36, 39, 40, 54, 55, 179, 185, 188, 189, 226, 243, **245**
  alternate 246
vulnerable 65, **167**, 174
walk the walk 163
war 61, 203
Wardley, Simon 200
waste 185
WDGLL 77
wealth 45, 234
Webber, Alan 6
Webo 233
weed 203
welcome 172
wellbeing 48, 162
wetware 237
whistleblower 174
whistleblowers 61
Whitaker, Todd 170
white and male 22
Whitehurst, Jim 17, 196
who 39, 43, 227
whole .. 47, 48, **164**, 173, 251
wholeness 231
why 35, 207, 226, 227
Wilbur, Ken 49
wisdom 23
woke 32

Index

work from here 182
work management ... 62, 202
workaholism 46
workplace 20, 47
   healthy **181**
workspace **181**

Yamada, Tadataka 162
Zanini, Michele 31, 154, 172, 232, 249
zebras 16
Zuckerberg, Mark 46

Printed in Great Britain
by Amazon